CHENG & TSUI

"Bringing Asia to the World"™

中文聽說讀寫

INTEGRATED CHINESE

Traditional Characters

1

Workbook

4th Edition

Yuehua Liu and Tao-chung Yao
Nyan-Ping Bi, Yaohua Shi, Liangyan Ge

Original Edition by Tao-chung Yao and Yuehua Liu
Yea-fen Chen, Liangyan Ge, Nyan-Ping Bi, Xiaojun Wang

CHENG & TSUI

"Bringing Asia to the World"™

Copyright © 2017, 2009, 2005, 1997 by
Cheng & Tsui Company, Inc.

Fourth Edition 2017
3rd Printing, 2022

25 24 23 22   3 4 5 6

ISBN: 978-1-62291-131-8 [Fourth Edition,
Traditional Characters]

Printed in the United States of America

The *Integrated Chinese* series includes
textbooks, workbooks, character
workbooks, teacher's resources, streaming
audio, video, and more. Visit chengtsui.co
for more information on the other
components of *Integrated Chinese*.

Publisher
JILL CHENG

Editorial Manager
BEN SHRAGGE

Editors
LEI WANG with LIJIE QIN, MIKE YONG, and
RANDY TELFER

Creative Director
CHRISTIAN SABOGAL

Interior Design
LIZ YATES

Illustrator
KATE PAPADAKI

Cheng & Tsui Company, Inc.
Phone (617) 988-2400 / (800) 554-1963
Fax (617) 426-3669
25 West Street
Boston, MA 02111-1213 USA
chengtsui.co

Contents

Preface

In designing the workbook exercises for *Integrated Chinese* (IC), we strove to give equal emphasis to the core language skills of listening, speaking, reading, and writing. For the new edition, we have also added *pinyin* and tone exercises for students to progressively improve their pronunciation, extra writing exercises to test their knowledge of Chinese characters, and lesson opener checklists so they can track their learning. Where appropriate, we have labeled the exercises as interpretive, interpersonal, or presentational according to the American Council on the Teaching of Foreign Languages (ACTFL) *21st Century Skills Map for World Languages*.

In addition to the print editions, the IC workbooks are also available online through the ChengTsui Web App (*Essential* and *Educator Editions*). In the digital format, the exercises are presented alongside the textbook content, and feature auto-grading capability. For more information and a free trial, visit chengtsui.co.

Organizational Principles

As with the textbooks, the IC workbooks do not follow one pedagogical methodology, but instead blend several effective teaching approaches. When accessed through the ChengTsui Web App, the workbooks are particularly suited for differentiated instruction, blended learning, and the flipped classroom. Here are some features that distinguish the IC workbooks:

Form and Function
The ultimate purpose of learning any language is to be able to communicate in that language. With that goal in mind, we pay equal attention to language form and function. In addition to traditional workbook exercise types (e.g., fill-in-the-blanks, sentence completion, translation, multiple choice), we include task-based assignments that equip students to handle real-life situations using accurate and appropriate language. These exercises provide linguistic context and are written to reflect idiomatic usage.

Visual Learning
Engaging learners through rich visuals is key to our pedagogy. To build a bridge between the classroom and the target language setting, we include a range of exercises centered on authentic materials. We also include illustration-based exercises that prompt students to answer questions directly in Chinese without going through the process of translation.

Learner-Centered Tasks
We believe that workbook exercises should not only align with the textbook, but also relate to students' lives. We include exercises that simulate daily life and reference culturally relevant topics and themes, including social media and globalization. We hope such open-ended exercises will actively engage students in the subject matter, and keep them interested in the language-learning process.

Differentiated Instruction
We have designed the exercises at different difficulty levels to suit varying curricular needs. Therefore, teachers should assign the exercises at their discretion; they may use some or all of them, in any sequence. Moreover, teachers may complement the workbook exercises with their own materials or with supplementary resources available at chengtsui.co.

Bringing It Together
Every five lessons, we provide a short cumulative review unit ("Bringing It Together") for students who wish to check their progress. These flexible units do not introduce any new learning materials, and can be included in or excluded from curricula according to individual needs.

For maximum flexibility in pacing, each lesson is divided into two parts corresponding to the lesson halves in the textbook. Teachers may spend two or three days teaching the first half and assigning students the associated exercises, then devote an equal amount of time to the second half and its exercises. Teachers may also give two separate vocabulary tests for the two readings to ease student workload.

The workbook lesson sections are as follows:

Listening Comprehension

All too often, listening comprehension is sacrificed in the formal classroom setting. Because of time constraints, students tend to focus their time and energy on mastering a few grammar points. We include a substantial number of listening comprehension exercises to remedy this imbalance. There are two categories of listening exercises; both can be done on students' own time or in the classroom. In either case, the instructor should review students' answers for accuracy.

The first group of listening exercises, which is placed at the beginning of this section, is based on the scenarios in the lesson. For the exercises to be meaningful, students should study the vocabulary list before listening to the recordings.

The second group of listening exercises is based on audio recordings of two or more short dialogues or narratives. These exercises are designed to give students extra practice on the vocabulary and grammar points introduced in the lesson. Some of the exercises, especially those that ask students to choose among several possible answers, are significantly more difficult than others. These exercises should be assigned towards the end of the lesson, after students have familiarized themselves with its content.

Streaming audio for the workbooks (and textbooks) is accessible at chengtsui.co.

Pinyin and Tone

This new section includes exercises that ask students to identify characters with the same initials or finals and write them in *pinyin*; and to indicate the tones of characters that are pronounced similarly. These exercises build on the foundation provided by the Basics section.

Speaking

As with Listening Comprehension, this section includes two groups of exercises. They should be assigned separately based on students' proficiency level.

To help students apply new vocabulary and grammar knowledge to meaningful communication, we first ask questions related to the dialogue or narrative, and then ask questions related to their own lives. These questions require a one- or two-sentence answer. By stringing together short questions and answers, students can construct their own short dialogues, practice in pairs, or take turns asking or answering questions.

As their confidence increases, students can progress to more difficult questions that invite them to express opinions on a number of topics. Typically, these questions are abstract, so they gradually teach students to express their opinions in longer conversations. As the school year progresses, these questions should take up more class discussion time. Because this second group of speaking exercises is quite challenging, it should be attempted only after students are well grounded in the lesson's grammar and vocabulary. Usually, this does not occur immediately after students have completed the first group of exercises.

Reading Comprehension

This section includes questions asking students to match terms, answer questions in English, or answer multiple-choice questions based on readings. There are also activities based on realia.

Writing and Grammar

Characters

These newly added exercises develop students' analytic ability by asking them to apply their knowledge of radicals and patterns. Where appropriate, space to practice writing characters is also provided.

Grammar and Usage

These drills and exercises are designed to solidify students' grasp of important grammar points. Through brief exchanges, students answer questions using specific grammatical forms, or are given sentences to complete. Because they must provide context for these exercises, students cannot treat them as simple mechanical repetition drills.

In the last three lessons, students are introduced to increasingly sophisticated and abstract vocabulary. Corresponding exercises help them to grasp the nuances of new words.

Translation

Translation has been a tool for language teaching through the ages, and positive student feedback confirms our belief in its continued importance. The exercises we have devised serve two primary functions: one, to have students apply specific grammatical structures; and two, to encourage students to build on their vocabulary. Ultimately, we believe this dual-pronged approach will enable students to realize that it takes more than just literal translation to convey an idea in a foreign language.

Writing Practice

This group of exercises is the culmination of the section, as it encourages students to express themselves through writing. Many of the topics overlap with those used in oral practice. We expect that students will find it easier to write what they have already learned to express orally.

Note: Prefaces to the previous editions of IC are available at chengtsui.co.

Basics

 Check off the following items as you learn them.

[ ] Simple finals

[ ] Initials

[ ] Compound finals

[ ] Tones

As you progress through the lesson, note what else you would like to learn to expand your knowledge of Chinese.

_____

_____

_____

Listen to the audio, then circle the correct answers.

A Simple Finals

1	a. *bā*	b. *bū*	**3**	a. *gū*	b. *gē*	**5** a. *lú*	b. *lǘ*
2	a. *kē*	b. *kā*	**4**	a. *pū*	b. *pō*		

B Initials

1	a. *pà*	b. *bà*	**10**	a. *kuì*	b. *huì*	**19**	a. *sè*	b. *shè*
2	a. *pí*	b. *bí*	**11**	a. *kǎi*	b. *hǎi*	**20**	a. *sè*	b. *cè*
3	a. *nán*	b. *mán*	**12**	a. *kuā*	b. *huā*	**21**	a. *zhǒng*	b. *jiǒng*
4	a. *fú*	b. *hú*	**13**	a. *jiān*	b. *qiān*	**22**	a. *shēn*	b. *sēn*
5	a. *tīng*	b. *dīng*	**14**	a. *yú*	b. *qú*	**23**	a. *rù*	b. *lù*
6	a. *tǒng*	b. *dǒng*	**15**	a. *xiāng*	b. *shāng*	**24**	a. *xiào*	b. *shào*
7	a. *nán*	b. *lán*	**16**	a. *chú*	b. *rú*	**25**	a. *qì*	b. *chì*
8	a. *niàn*	b. *liàn*	**17**	a. *zhá*	b. *zá*			
9	a. *gàn*	b. *kàn*	**18**	a. *zì*	b. *cì*			

C Compound Finals

1	a. *tuō*	b. *tōu*	**10**	a. *píng*	b. *pín*	**19**	a. *téng*	b. *tóng*
2	a. *guǒ*	b. *gǒu*	**11**	a. *làn*	b. *luàn*	**20**	a. *kēng*	b. *kōng*
3	a. *duò*	b. *dòu*	**12**	a. *huán*	b. *hán*	**21**	a. *pàn*	b. *pàng*
4	a. *diū*	b. *dōu*	**13**	a. *fèng*	b. *fèn*	**22**	a. *fǎn*	b. *fǎng*
5	a. *liú*	b. *lóu*	**14**	a. *bèng*	b. *bèn*	**23**	a. *mín*	b. *míng*
6	a. *yǒu*	b. *yǔ*	**15**	a. *lún*	b. *léng*	**24**	a. *pēn*	b. *pān*
7	a. *nǔ*	b. *nǚ*	**16**	a. *bīn*	b. *bīng*	**25**	a. *rén*	b. *rán*
8	a. *lú*	b. *lǘ*	**17**	a. *kěn*	b. *kǔn*			
9	a. *yuán*	b. *yán*	**18**	a. *héng*	b. *hóng*			

D Tones: First and Fourth (Level and Falling)

1	a. *bō*	b. *bò*	**5**	a. *qū*	b. *qù*	**9**	a. *xià*	b. *xiā*
2	a. *pān*	b. *pàn*	**6**	a. *sì*	b. *sī*	**10**	a. *yā*	b. *yà*
3	a. *wù*	b. *wū*	**7**	a. *fēi*	b. *fèi*			
4	a. *tà*	b. *tā*	**8**	a. *duì*	b. *duī*			

E Tones: Second and Third (Rising and Low)

1	a. *mǎi*	b. *mái*	**5**	a. *wú*	b. *wǔ*	**9**	a. *féi*	b. *fěi*
2	a. *fǎng*	b. *fáng*	**6**	a. *bǎ*	b. *bá*	**10**	a. *láo*	b. *lǎo*
3	a. *tú*	b. *tǔ*	**7**	a. *zhǐ*	b. *zhí*			
4	a. *gé*	b. *gě*	**8**	a. *huī*	b. *huí*			

F All Four Tones

1	a. bà	b. bā	**10**	a. mào	b. máo	**19**	a. zhèng	b. zhēng
2	a. pí	b. pì	**11**	a. bǔ	b. bù	**20**	a. chòu	b. chóu
3	a. méi	b. měi	**12**	a. kuàng	b. kuāng	**21**	a. shuāi	b. shuài
4	a. wēn	b. wěn	**13**	a. jú	b. jǔ	**22**	a. wǒ	b. wò
5	a. zǎo	b. zāo	**14**	a. qiáng	b. qiāng	**23**	a. yào	b. yáo
6	a. yōu	b. yóu	**15**	a. xián	b. xiān	**24**	a. huī	b. huì
7	a. guāng	b. guǎng	**16**	a. yǒng	b. yòng	**25**	a. rú	b. rù
8	a. cí	b. cǐ	**17**	a. zú	b. zū			
9	a. qì	b. qí	**18**	a. suī	b. suí			

G Comprehensive Exercise

1	a. jiā	b. zhā	**10**	a. dǒu	b. duǒ	**19**	a. liè	b. lüè
2	a. chuí	b. qué	**11**	a. duǒ	b. zuǒ	**20**	a. jīn	b. zhēn
3	a. chǎng	b. qiǎng	**12**	a. mǎi	b. měi	**21**	a. xiǔ	b. shǒu
4	a. xū	b. shū	**13**	a. chóu	b. qiú	**22**	a. kǔn	b. hěn
5	a. shuǐ	b. xuě	**14**	a. yuè	b. yè	**23**	a. shǎo	b. xiǎo
6	a. zǎo	b. zhǎo	**15**	a. jiǔ	b. zhǒu	**24**	a. zhǎng	b. jiǎng
7	a. zǎo	b. cǎo	**16**	a. nǔ	b. nǚ	**25**	a. qū	b. chū
8	a. sōu	b. shōu	**17**	a. zhú	b. jú			
9	a. tōu	b. tuō	**18**	a. jī	b. zì			

Tone Combination Exercise

Audio

Listen to the words in the audio, then indicate the tones with 1 (first tone), 2 (second tone), 3 (third tone), 4 (fourth tone), or 0 (neutral tone) in the spaces provided. Note that the images in exercise A depict the meaning of the words.

A Multisyllabic Words

1

2

3

4

5

6

_____

Basics

3

7

_____

9

_____

11

_____

8

_____

10

_____

12

_____

B Disyllabic Words

1 _____

2 _____

3 _____

4 _____

5 _____

6 _____

7 _____

8 _____

9 _____

10 _____

11 _____

12 _____

13 _____

14 _____

15 _____

16 _____

17 _____

18 _____

19 _____

20 _____

21 _____

22 _____

23 _____

24 _____

25 _____

26 _____

27 _____

28 _____

29 _____

30 _____

Audio

Initials and Simple Finals

Listen to the audio, then fill in the blanks with the appropriate initials or simple finals.

A 1. __a   2. p__   3. __u   4. l__

B 1. f__   2. n__   3. __i   4. __u

C 1. __a   2. l__   3. l__   4. __u

D 1. __u   2. t__   3. n__   4. n__

E 1. __e   2. __u   3. __a

F	1. *g*___	2. *k*___	3. *h*___	
G	1. ___*u*	2. ___*i*	3. ___*u*	
H	1. *j*___	2. *q*___	3. *x*___	
I	1. ___*a*	2. ___*e*	3. ___*i*	4. ___*u*
J	1. ___*u*	2. *c*___	3. ___*u*	4. ___*i*
K	1. ___*i*	2. *s*___	3. ___*a*	4. *q*___
L	1. ___*a*	2. ___*i*	3. *s*___	4. ___*u*
M	1. *c*___	2. ___*i*	3. ___*u*	4. ___*a*
N	1. ___*u*	2. *r*___	3. *ch*___	4. ___*e*

Audio

Tones

Listen to the audio, then add the correct tone marks.

A	1. *he*	2. *ma*	3. *pa*	4. *di*
B	1. *nü*	2. *re*	3. *chi*	4. *zhu*
C	1. *mo*	2. *qu*	3. *ca*	4. *si*
D	1. *tu*	2. *fo*	3. *ze*	4. *ju*
E	1. *lü*	2. *bu*	3. *xi*	4. *shi*
F	1. *gu*	2. *se*	3. *ci*	4. *ku*
G	1. *mang*	2. *quan*	3. *yuan*	4. *yue*
H	1. *yi*	2. *er*	3. *san*	4. *si*
I	1. *ba*	2. *qi*	3. *liu*	4. *wu*
J	1. *jiu*	2. *shi*	3. *tian*	4. *jin*
K	1. *mu*	2. *shui*	3. *huo*	4. *ren*
L	1. *yu*	2. *zhuang*	3. *qun*	4. *zhong*

Audio

Compound Finals

Listen to the audio, then fill in the blanks with the appropriate compound finals.

1	a. *zh*___	b. *t*___	c. *k*___	d. *j*___
2	a. *x*___	b. *q*___	c. *j*___	d. *d*___
3	a. *x*___	b. *zh*___	c. *t*___	d. *g*___
4	a. *sh*___	b. *b*___	c. *z*___	d. *q*___
5	a. *j*___	b. *d*___	c. *x*___	d. *ch*___
6	a. *zh*___	b. *l*___	c. *k*___	d. *j*___
7	a. *s*___	b. *x*___	c. *p*___	d. *ch*___

Compound Finals and Tones

Listen to the audio, then fill in the blanks with the appropriate compound finals and tone marks.

1 a. *m*___   b. *zh*___   c. *sh*___   d. *zh*___

2 a. *sh*___   b. *t*___   c. *l*___   d. *b*___

3 a. *s*___   b. *j*___   c. *k*___   d. *d*___

4 a. *l*___   b. *q*___   c. *t*___   d. *x*___

5 a. *f*___   b. *p*___   c. *x*___   d. *j*___

6 a. *b*___   b. *j*___   c. *q*___   d. *t*___

7 a. *l*___   b. *g*___   c. *q*___   d. *x*___

Audio

Neutral Tone

Listen to the words in the audio one at a time, then indicate the tones with 1 (first tone), 2 (second tone), 3 (third tone), 4 (fourth tone), or 0 (neutral tone).

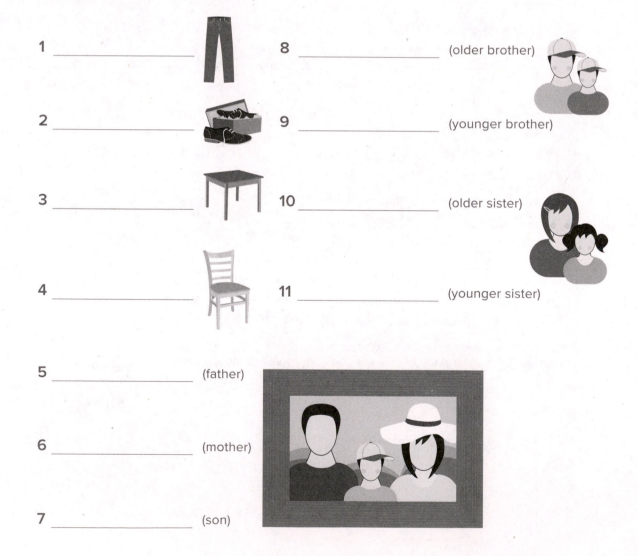

1 _____

2 _____

3 _____

4 _____

5 _____ (father)

6 _____ (mother)

7 _____ (son)

8 _____ (older brother)

9 _____ (younger brother)

10 _____ (older sister)

11 _____ (younger sister)

Initials, Finals, and Tones: Disyllabic Words

Listen to the audio, then circle the correct answers.

1	a. *làoshī*	b. *lǎoshī*	c. *lǎoshí*	(teacher)
2	a. *nǚ'ér*	b. *nǚ'èr*	c. *nǚ'ér*	(daughter)
3	a. *zhàopiàn*	b. *zhāopiàn*	c. *zháopiàn*	(photograph)
4	a. *wànfàn*	b. *wǎnfàn*	c. *wǎnfàn*	(dinner)
5	a. *shēngrì*	b. *shéngrì*	c. *shěngrì*	(birthday)
6	a. *zāijiàn*	b. *zàijiàn*	c. *záijiàn*	(goodbye)
7	a. *xuéshēng*	b. *xuèsheng*	c. *xuésheng*	(student)
8	a. *diànyǐng*	b. *diānyǐng*	c. *diànyìng*	(movie)
9	a. *zuòtiān*	b. *zuótiān*	c. *zuótiàn*	(yesterday)
10	a. *suírán*	b. *suīrán*	c. *suīràn*	(although)
11	a. *xièxiè*	b. *shèshe*	c. *xièxie*	(thanks)
12	a. *kāfēi*	b. *káfēi*	c. *kāifēi*	(coffee)
13	a. *kēlè*	b. *kělè*	c. *kělà*	(cola)
14	a. *píngcháng*	b. *pēngchán*	c. *píngchèng*	(normally)
15	a. *gōngzuò*	b. *gōngzhuò*	c. *gōngzòu*	(work)
16	a. *piàoliàng*	b. *piāoliang*	c. *piàoliang*	(pretty)
17	a. *wèntì*	b. *wèntí*	c. *wěntí*	(questions)
18	a. *rōngyì*	b. *lóngyì*	c. *róngyì*	(easy)
19	a. *kāishǐ*	b. *kāixǐ*	c. *kāisǐ*	(begin)
20	a. *lòudiǎn*	b. *liùdiǎn*	c. *liùdǎn*	(six o'clock)

Initials, Finals, and Tones: Monosyllabic Words

Listen to the audio, then transcribe what you hear into *pinyin* with tone marks.

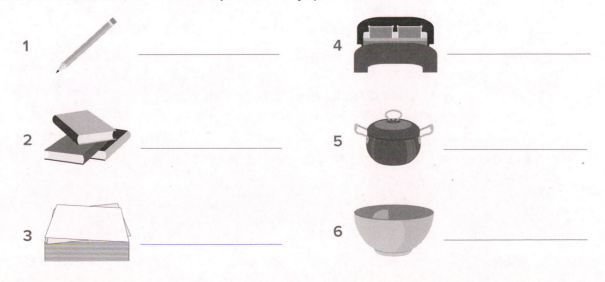

1 _____

2 _____

3 _____

4 _____

5 _____

6 _____

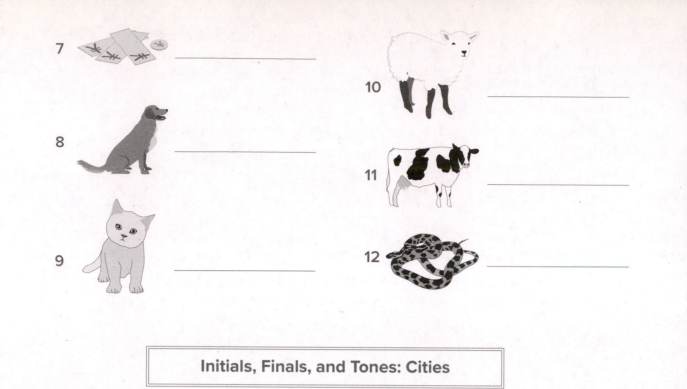

7 _____

8 _____

9 _____

10 _____

11 _____

12 _____

Initials, Finals, and Tones: Cities

Listen to the *pinyin* words in the left column, then connect them with the corresponding cities in the right column, e.g.:

Mài'āmì   ⟶   Miami

1 ___ *Bōshìdùn*   a.   Venice

2 ___ *Lúndūn*   b.   Toronto

3 ___ *Niǔyuē*   c.   Boston

4 ___ *Bālí*   d.   Chicago

5 ___ *Zhījiāgē*   e.   Seattle

6 ___ *Běijīng*   f.   New York

7 ___ *Luòshānjī*   g.   Paris

8 ___ *Duōlúnduō*   h.   London

9 ___ *Xīyǎtú*   i.   Beijing

10 ___ *Wēinísī*   j.   Los Angeles

Initials, Finals, and Tones: Countries

Listen to the audio, transcribe what you hear into *pinyin* with tone marks, then identify the countries, e.g.:

Rìběn   ⟶   Japan

1 _____ ⟶ _____

2 _____ ⟶ _____

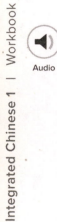

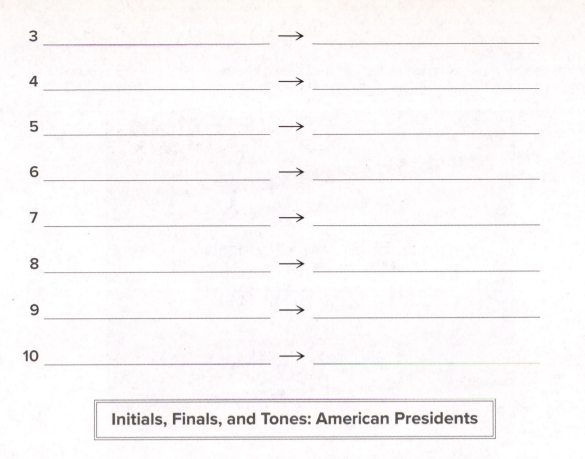

3 _____ → _____

4 _____ → _____

5 _____ → _____

6 _____ → _____

7 _____ → _____

8 _____ → _____

9 _____ → _____

10 _____ → _____

Initials, Finals, and Tones: American Presidents

Audio

Listen to the audio, transcribe what you hear into *pinyin* with tone marks, then identify the American presidents.

1 _____ → _____

2 _____ → _____

3 _____ → _____

4 _____ → _____

5 _____ → _____

6 _____ → _____

7 _____ → _____

8 _____ → _____

9 _____ → _____

10 _____ → _____

The tones for the three characters on the sign are 2, 3, and 4, respectively. Can you pronounce what's on the sign? If you can, then you know how to say "emergency room" in Chinese.

問好
Greetings

 Check off the following items as you learn them.

Useful Expressions

- [ ] Hello!
- [ ] What's your name?
- [ ] My name is _____ (your name).
- [ ] I'm a student.
- [ ] I'm _____ (your nationality).

Cultural Norms

- [ ] Polite introductions
- [ ] Standard forms of address
- [ ] Common family names
- [ ] Proper name order

As you progress through the lesson, note other useful expressions and cultural norms you would like to learn.

_____

_____

_____

Dialogue 1: Exchanging Greetings

🔊 **Audio**

Listening Comprehension

A Listen to the Textbook Dialogue 1 audio, then circle the most appropriate choice. INTERPRETIVE

1 What does the man first say to the woman?
- a What's your name?
- b I'm Mr. Wang.
- c Are you Miss Li?
- d How do you do?

2 What is the woman's full name?
- a Wang Peng
- b Li You
- c Xing Li
- d Jiao Liyou

3 What is the man's full name?
- a Wang Peng
- b Li You
- c Xing Wang
- d Jiao Wangpeng

B Listen to the Workbook Dialogue 1* audio, then circle the most appropriate choice. INTERPRETIVE

1 These two people are
- a saying goodbye to each other.
- b asking each other's name.
- c greeting each other.
- d asking each other's nationality.

C Listen to the Workbook Dialogue 2 audio, then circle the most appropriate choice. INTERPRETIVE

1 The two speakers are most likely
- a brother and sister.
- b father and daughter.
- c two old friends being reunited.
- d strangers getting acquainted.

2 These two people are
- a Mr. Li and Miss You.
- b Mr. Li and Miss Li.
- c Mr. Wang and Miss You.
- d Mr. Wang and Miss Li.

---

*In Listening Comprehension, references to Workbook Dialogues and Narratives correspond to audio recordings of new Chinese texts, not the dialogues and narratives from the textbook.

Pinyin and Tone

A Identify the characters with the same initials (either *x* or *sh*) and write them in *pinyin*.

先　什　姓　小

1　*x:* _____

2　*sh:* _____

B Compare the tones of these characters. Indicate the tones with 1 (first tone), 2 (second tone), 3 (third tone), 4 (fourth tone), or 0 (neutral tone).

1　你 _____　問 _____

2　我 _____　叫 _____

3　什 _____　麼 _____

Speaking

A Answer these questions in Chinese based on Textbook Dialogue 1. PRESENTATIONAL

1　How does Mr. Wang greet Miss Li?

2　What is Miss Li's reply?

3　How does Mr. Wang ask what Miss Li's family name is?

4　What is Mr. Wang's given name?

5　How does Mr. Wang ask what Miss Li's given name is?

6　What is Miss Li's given name?

B In pairs, role-play meeting someone for the first time. Try to complete the following tasks in Chinese. INTERPERSONAL

1　Exchange greetings with each other.

2　Ask each other's family name and given name.

A Read these Chinese sentences: 你好，先生。請問你貴姓？Then mark these statements true or false. **INTERPRETIVE**

1 _____ The question is addressed to a man.

2 _____ The speaker is talking to his/her friend.

3 _____ The sentence occurs at the end of a conversation.

4 _____ We do not know the addressee's family name.

B Read these Chinese sentences: 小姐，你好。我姓李，叫李朋。你呢？Then mark these statements true or false. **INTERPRETIVE**

1 _____ The speaker is talking to a man.

2 _____ We don't know whether the speaker is a man or a woman.

3 _____ We know the speaker's full name.

4 _____ The speaker knows the addressee's full name.

Writing and Grammar

A Which of these characters are based on the left-right pattern, and which on the top-bottom pattern? After filling in the answers, write the characters in the spaces provided.

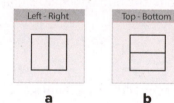

Left - Right **a**

Top - Bottom **b**

1 ___ 你

2 ___ 貴

3 ___ 請

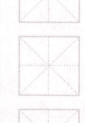

4 ___ 什

5 ___ 李

6 ___ 朋

B Rearrange these Chinese words into a complete sentence. Use the English in parentheses as a clue. PRESENTATIONAL

1 叫 | 名字 | 你 | 請問 | 什麼

(May I ask what your name is?)

_____

2 王朋 | 我 | 叫

(My name is Wang Peng.)

_____

3 姓 | 李 | 我

(My family name is Li.)

_____

C Rewrite and answer these questions in characters. PRESENTATIONAL

1 _Nǐ hǎo!_

_____

2 _Nǐ guì xìng?_

_____

3 _Nǐ jiào shénme míngzi?_

_____

D Translate these sentences into Chinese. PRESENTATIONAL

1 Hi, Mr. Wang.

_____

2 **Q:** May I ask what your family name is?

_____

A: My family name is Li. My name is Li You.

_____

E Write your Chinese name, if you have one, in characters. If you don't, come up with one (ask your teacher for help if needed).

_____

Dialogue 2: Where Are You From?

Audio

Listening Comprehension

A Listen to the Textbook Dialogue 2 audio, then mark these statements true or false. Quote the key sentence from the dialogue, in either *pinyin* or characters, to support your answer. INTERPRETIVE

1 _____ Miss Li is a student.

_____

2 _____ Mr. Wang is a teacher.

_____

3 _____ Mr. Wang is American.

_____

4 _____ Miss Li is Chinese.

_____

B Listen to the Workbook Dialogue 1 audio, then mark these statements true or false. INTERPRETIVE

1 _____ Both the man and the woman are Chinese.

2 _____ Both the man and the woman are American.

3 _____ The man is Chinese and the woman is American.

4 _____ The man is American and the woman is Chinese.

C Listen to the Workbook Dialogue 2 audio, then mark these statements true or false. INTERPRETIVE

1 _____ Both the man and the woman are teachers.

2 _____ Both the man and the woman are students.

3 _____ The man is a teacher. The woman is a student.

4 _____ The man is a student. The woman is a teacher.

Pinyin and Tone

A Identify the characters with the same initials (either *x* or *sh*) and write them in *pinyin*.

先　師　什　姓　是　小

1 *x:* _____

2 *sh:* _____

B Compare the tones of these characters. Indicate the tones with 1 (first tone), 2 (second tone), 3 (third tone), 4 (fourth tone), or 0 (neutral tone).

1 是 _____ 師 _____

Speaking

A Answer these questions in Chinese based on Textbook Dialogue 2. PRESENTATIONAL

   1 How does Miss Li ask whether Mr. Wang is a teacher or not?

   2 Is Mr. Wang a teacher?

   3 Is Miss Li a teacher?

   4 What is Mr. Wang's nationality?

   5 What is Miss Li's nationality?

B You meet a Chinese person on campus. Ask politely in Chinese whether he/she is a teacher. INTERPERSONAL

C You've just met a foreign student who can speak Chinese. INTERPERSONAL

   1 Ask whether he/she is Chinese.

   2 Tell him/her that you are American.

D Introduce yourself in Chinese to your class. Tell your classmates what your Chinese name is and whether you are a student. PRESENTATIONAL

Reading Comprehension

A Match the sentences in the left column with the appropriate responses in the right column.
INTERPRETIVE

1 _____ 你好！   a 是，我是老師。

2 _____ 您貴姓？   b 不，我是中國人。

3 _____ 你是美國人嗎？   c 我也是學生。

4 _____ 你是老師嗎？   d 我姓李。

5 _____ 我是學生，你呢？   e 你好！

B After reading this passage, fill in the chart, then answer the questions that follow by circling the most appropriate choice. INTERPRETIVE

王先生叫王師中。王師中是紐約人，不是中國人。王師中是學生，不是老師。李小姐是北京人，叫李美生。李美生是老師，不是學生。

	Gender	Given Name	Nationality	Occupation	Hometown
王先生					
李小姐					

1 If you were the man's close friend, how would you normally address him?
   a Wang Xiansheng
   b Xiansheng Wang
   c Wang
   d Shizhong

2 If you were introduced to the woman for the first time, with which term would it be most appropriate to address her?

a Li Xiaojie

b Xiaojie Li

c Li Meisheng

d Meisheng

C Read this dialogue, then answer the questions in English. INTERPRETIVE

李先生：請問，你是王老師嗎？

王小姐：是，我是。你是⋯⋯

李先生：王老師，你好。我姓李，叫李大中。

王小姐：李大中，李大中⋯⋯ò,李老師，是你ya⋯⋯你好，你好。

1 Is this a dialogue between a teacher and a student?

_____

2 Are the two speakers very familiar with each other?

_____

3 What tone of voice does the interjection "ò" bring to the dialogue?

_____

4 What tone of voice does the particle "ya" bring to the dialogue?

_____

D On these three Chinese business cards, underline the characters that are family names. INTERPRETIVE

美國夏威夷大學東亞語文系教授

李 英 哲
YINGCHE LI

EAST ASIAN LANGUAGES AND LITERATURES
UNIVERSITY OF HAWAII
HONOLULU, HAWAII 96822
U.S.A

TEL: (808) 956-xxxx(0)
FAX: (808) 956-xxxx

中外合資
常州華潤裝飾工程有限公司
CHANGZHOU HUA RUN DECORATION ENGINEERING CO. LTD

王 德 中
WANG   DE   ZHONG
董事 副總經理

地址： 中國常州勞動中路42號
ADD: NO42 LAO DONG RD(M) CHANGZHOU
電話 TEL: 8824xxxx 881xxxx
傳真 FAX: 0519–882xxxx
電掛 CABLE: 5000 郵編 P.C:213001
宅電 HOME:662xxxx

台北美國學校

外語系中文部主任

王 智 寧

校址：台北市士林區中山北路巷六段八○○號
電話：八七三—x x x 轉二四○
傳真：八七三—x x x x
住宅：台北市中山北路七段114巷57號三樓
電話：/傳真：（〇二）八七—x x x x x

E Review these two Chinese business cards, then answer the questions in English. INTERPRETIVE

外語教學與研究出版社
北京外語音像出版社

王　偉
音像中心

地址：北京市西三環北路19號（北京外國語大學）
電話：(010)6891 XXXX
手機：13671 XXXX   郵編：100089

美國在台協會華語學校

王　俊　仁

台北市陽明山山仔后
愛富三街長生巷5號

電話：(02) 2861- XXXX
傳真：(02) 2861- XXXX

1 What are the card owners' family names?

2 Which business card's owner works in Beijing?

A Which of these characters are based on the unitary pattern, and which on the enclosing pattern? After filling in the answers, write the characters in the spaces provided.

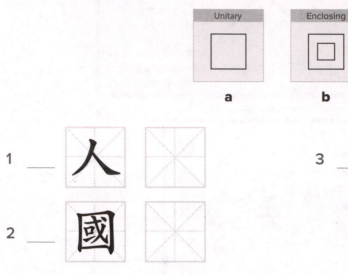

B Rewrite these sentences in characters. PRESENTATIONAL

1 *Qǐng wèn, nǐ shì xuésheng ma?*

_____

2 *Wǒ shì Zhōngguó rén. Nǐ ne?*

_____

3 *Wǒ bú xìng Wáng, wǒ xìng Lǐ.*

_____

4 *Nǐ shì lǎoshī, wǒ shì xuésheng.*

_____

5 *Nǐ shì Měiguó rén, wǒ yě shì Měiguó rén.*

_____

C Rearrange these Chinese words into sentences, using the English in parentheses as clues. PRESENTATIONAL

1 姓 | 王 | 嗎 | 你

(Is your family name Wang?)

_____

2 嗎 | 是 | 你 | 學生 | 中國

(Are you a Chinese student?)

_____

3 北京 | 是 | 人 | 我 | 不

(I am not from Beijing.)

_____

4 小姐 | 先生 | 紐約人 | 紐約人 | 王 | 李 | 也 | 是 | 是

(Miss Wang is a New Yorker. Mr. Li is also from New York.)

_____

D Answer these questions in Chinese according to your own circumstances. INTERPERSONAL

1 Q: 你是學生嗎？

A: _____

2 Q: 你是北京人嗎？

A: _____

3 Q: 李小姐是美國人。你呢？

A: _____

4 Q: 王先生是中國學生。你呢？

A: _____

E Write out the questions to which these statements are the appropriate answers, following the example below. PRESENTATIONAL

我是學生。

你是學生嗎？

1　我是美國人。_____

2　我姓李。_____

3　王老師是北京人。_____

4　李小姐不是老師。_____

5　我也是學生。_____

F Connect these clauses to form compound sentences using 也, following the example below.
PRESENTATIONAL

李友是學生。｜王朋是學生。

李友是學生，王朋也是學生。

1　你是美國人。｜我是美國人。

_____

2　李小姐不是中國人。｜李先生不是中國人。

_____

3　你不姓王。｜我不姓王。

_____

4　王先生不是紐約人。｜李小姐不是紐約人。

_____

G Complete this conversation in characters based on the information given. PRESENTATIONAL

Student A: _____ 。

Student B: _____ 。

Student A: _____ ， _____ ？

Student B: 我姓王。

Student A: _____ ？

Student B: 我叫王京。

Student A: _____ , _____ ?

Student B: 不，我不是，我是中國人。

Student A: _____ , _____ ?

Student B: 我也是。

H Translate these sentences into Chinese. PRESENTATIONAL

1 Q: Is Mr. Wang Chinese?

_____

A: Yes, Mr. Wang is from Beijing.

_____

2 Q: Li You is a student. How about you?

_____

A: I am also a student.

_____

3 Q: I am from New York. Are you from New York, too?

_____

A: No, I am from Beijing.

_____

4 Q: My family name is Wang. Is your family name Wang also?

_____

A: No, my family name is not Wang. My family name is Li.

_____

I Write a self-introduction in Chinese by filling in the blanks. PRESENTATIONAL

你好！我姓_____，叫_____。
我是_____人，不是_____人。
我是_____，不是_____。

家庭
Family

✔ Check off the following items as you learn them.

Useful Expressions

- [ ] There are _____ (number) people in my family.
- [ ] Who is this girl/boy?
- [ ] He/she is my older brother/sister.
- [ ] I don't have any brothers/sisters.
- [ ] My dad/mom is a _____ (profession).

Cultural Norms

- [ ] Kinship terms
- [ ] Family structure
- [ ] Business card etiquette

As you progress through the lesson, note other useful expressions and cultural norms you would like to learn.

_____

_____

_____

Dialogue 1: Looking at a Family Photo

Listening Comprehension

A   Listen to the Textbook Dialogue 1 audio, then mark these statements true or false. INTERPRETIVE

1   _____   Wang Peng knows the people in the picture.

2   _____   Gao Wenzhong doesn't have any older sisters.

3   _____   Gao Wenzhong's parents are in the picture.

4   _____   Gao Wenzhong's younger brother is also in the picture.

5   _____   Gao Wenzhong's older brother doesn't have any daughters.

B   Listen to the Workbook Dialogue 1 audio, then circle the most appropriate choice. INTERPRETIVE

1   Who are the people in the picture?

    a   The woman's mother and younger sister.

    b   The woman's mother and older sister.

    c   The woman's older sister and younger sister.

    d   The woman's mother and her mother's sister.

C   Listen to the Workbook Dialogue 2 audio, then circle the most appropriate choice. INTERPRETIVE

1   Which of the following statements is true?

    a   Wang Jing is the woman's sister.

    b   Wang Jing is the man's daughter.

    c   Wang Jing is not related to Mr. Wang.

    d   Wang Jing is not related to the woman.

Pinyin and Tone

A Identify the characters with the same initials (either *j* or *zh*) and write them in *pinyin*.

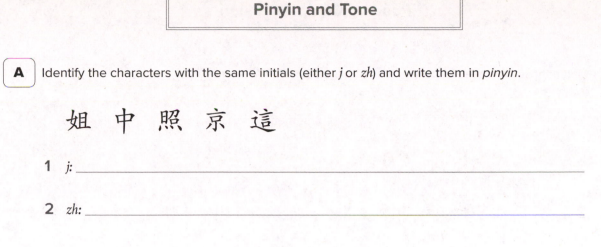

姐　中　照　京　這

1 *j:* _____

2 *zh:* _____

B Compare the tones of these characters. Indicate the tones with 1 (first tone), 2 (second tone), 3 (third tone), 4 (fourth tone), or 0 (neutral tone).

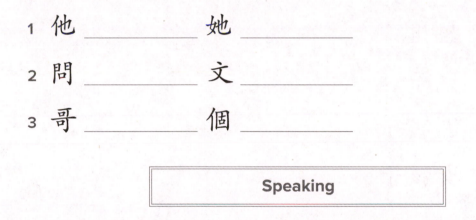

1 他 _____ 她 _____

2 問 _____ 文 _____

3 哥 _____ 個 _____

Speaking

A Answer these questions in Chinese based on Textbook Dialogue 1. PRESENTATIONAL

1 Whose photo is on the wall?

2 Who is the young lady in the picture?

3 Who is the boy in the picture?

4 Does Gao Wenzhong's older brother have a son or a daughter?

B Using a picture found online, introduce your favorite cartoon or celebrity family to a partner. Then ask your partner if there are any older sisters or younger brothers in the family. INTERPERSONAL

A Match these Chinese words with their English equivalents. INTERPRETIVE

1 _____ 爸爸   a   mother

2 _____ 大哥   b   boy

3 _____ 弟弟   c   older sister

4 _____ 女兒   d   eldest/oldest brother

5 _____ 媽媽   e   younger brother

6 _____ 姐姐   f   son

7 _____ 兒子   g   girl

8 _____ 男孩子   h   father

9 _____ 女孩子   i   daughter

B Match the questions on the left with the appropriate replies on the right. INTERPRETIVE

1 _____ 這個人是誰？   a   我沒有弟弟。

2 _____ 這是你的照片嗎？   b   這是我爸爸。

3 _____ 這個男孩子是
你弟弟嗎？   c   他有兒子，
沒有女兒。

4 _____ 你妹妹是學生嗎？   d   不是，他是王
老師的兒子。

5 _____ 李先生有女兒嗎？   e   是我的。

6 _____ 你有弟弟嗎？   f   她是學生。

C Read this dialogue, then circle the most appropriate choice. **INTERPRETIVE**

王朋：李友，這個女孩子是你嗎？

李友：不，她是我媽媽。

王朋：你媽媽？這個男孩子是你爸爸嗎？

李友：不是，他是我媽媽的大哥。

1 What are the speakers doing while talking?

a looking at a picture of Wang Peng

b looking at a picture taken many years ago

c looking at a picture they took yesterday

d looking at Li You's parent's picture

2 Who is in the picture?

a Wang Peng and Li You

b Li You and her mother

c Wang Peng and Li You's mother

d Li You's mother and Li You's uncle

Writing and Grammar

A Which of these characters are based on the left-right pattern, and which on the unitary pattern? After filling in the answers, write the characters in the spaces provided.

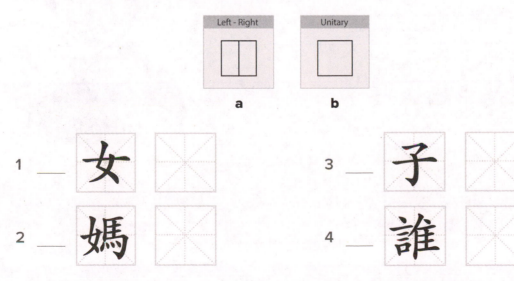

Left - Right	Unitary
a	b

1 ___ 女

2 ___ 媽

3 ___ 子

4 ___ 誰

5 ___

7 ___

6 ___ 他 ▨

B Fill in the blanks with 這 or 那 based on the prompt.

1 You point to a person standing about thirty feet away, and say:

_____ 個人是我的老師，他是北京人。

2 You are holding a family photo in your hand, and say:

_____ 是我爸爸，_____ 是我媽媽。

3 You look down the hallway and recognize someone, and say:

_____ 個人叫李生，是李友的爸爸。

4 You introduce to your friend a girl sitting at the same table, and say:

_____ 是李先生的女兒，李小約。

C Answer these questions based on the image. INTERPERSONAL

1 這個人是誰？／他是誰？

_____

2 這個人是中國人嗎？／
他是中國人嗎？

_____

D | Answer these questions in Chinese according to your own circumstances. INTERPERSONAL

1 你有姐姐嗎？

_____

2 你有弟弟嗎？

_____

3 你爸爸叫什麼名字？

_____

4 你媽媽是老師嗎？

_____

E | Focus on the underlined words, and write out the questions to which these statements are the appropriate answers. Follow the example below. PRESENTATIONAL

他是王朋。

誰是王朋？

1 這是王老師的照片。

_____

2 那個男孩子是王朋。

_____

F | Translate these sentences into Chinese. PRESENTATIONAL

1 Q: Little Wang, is this your photograph?

_____

A: This is not my photograph.

_____

2 **Q:** Mr. Wang doesn't have any sons. How about Mr. Li?

_____

    A: He doesn't, either.

_____

3 **Q:** Who is this young lady?

_____

    A: She's my older sister.

_____

4 **Q:** Does your oldest brother have a son?

_____

    A: No, he doesn't have any sons, nor does he have any daughters.

_____

G Write a summary of a well-known family, including names of family members and their relationships to each other. PRESENTATIONAL

_____

_____

_____

_____

Dialogue 2: Discussing Family

Listening Comprehension	

A   Listen to the Textbook Dialogue 2 audio, then circle the most appropriate choice. INTERPRETIVE

1   How many people are there in Bai Ying'ai's family?

    a   three

    b   four

    c   five

    d   six

2   How many people are there in Li You's family?

    a   three

    b   four

    c   five

    d   six

3   How many younger sisters does Bai Ying'ai have?

    a   none

    b   one

    c   two

    d   three

4   How many older sisters does Li You have?

    a   none

    b   one

    c   two

    d   three

5   How many older brothers does Bai Ying'ai have?

    a   none

    b   one

    c   two

    d   three

6   How many younger brothers does Bai Ying'ai have?

    a   none

    b   one

    c   two

    d   three

7   How many children do Bai Ying'ai's parents have?

    a   two

    b   three

    c   four

    d   five

8 How many sons do Li You's parents have?

    a   none

    b   one

    c   two

    d   three

9 What is Bai Ying'ai's father's occupation?

    a   lawyer

    b   teacher

    c   doctor

    d   student

10 What is Li You's mother's occupation?

    a   lawyer

    b   teacher

    c   doctor

    d   student

B Listen to the Workbook Dialogue 1 audio, then circle the most appropriate choice. INTERPRETIVE

1 Which of the following is true?

    a   Both the man and the woman have older brothers.

    b   Both the man and the woman have younger brothers.

    c   The man has an older brother but no younger brothers.

    d   The man has a younger brother but no older brothers.

2 The woman laughs at the end of the conversation because

    a   neither the man nor she herself has any younger brothers.

    b   neither the man nor she herself has any older brothers.

    c   the man failed to count himself as his older brother's younger brother.

    d   the man failed to count himself as his younger brother's older brother.

C Listen to the Workbook Dialogue 2 audio, then circle the most appropriate choice. INTERPRETIVE

1 What is the occupation of the man's mother?

    a   teacher

    b   student

    c   doctor

    d   lawyer

2 What is the occupation of the woman's father?

    a   teacher

    b   student

    c   doctor

    d   lawyer

D Listen to the Workbook Dialogue 3 audio, then circle the most appropriate choice. INTERPRETIVE

1 How many brothers does the woman have?

   a   one

   b   two

   c   three

   d   four

2 How many daughters do the woman's parents have?

   a   one

   b   two

   c   three

   d   four

3 How many people in the woman's family are older than herself?

   a   two

   b   three

   c   four

   d   five

4 How many people in the man's family are younger than himself?

   a   none

   b   one

   c   two

   d   three

5 When talking about the number of people in his family, the man forgot to include

   a   his older brother.

   b   his younger sister.

   c   his younger brother.

   d   himself.

Pinyin and Tone

A Identify the characters with the same finals (either *uo* or *ou*) and write them in *pinyin*.

口　國　都　有　我

1 *uo:* _____

2 *ou:* _____

B Compare the tones of these characters. Indicate the tones with 1 (first tone), 2 (second tone), 3 (third tone), 4 (fourth tone), or 0 (neutral tone).

1 妹 _____ 沒 _____

2 做 _____ 作 _____

Speaking

A Answer these questions in Chinese based on Textbook Dialogue 2. PRESENTATIONAL

1 How many people are there in Bai Ying'ai's family?

2 How many brothers and sisters does Li You have?

3 What is Bai Ying'ai's father's occupation?

4 What are Bai Ying'ai's mother's and Li You's mother's occupations?

5 How many people are there in Li You's family?

B Using a family portrait, introduce your family members to the class. PRESENTATIONAL

C In pairs, share family portraits and ask questions about the identity and occupations of family members. INTERPERSONAL

Reading Comprehension

A Mr. Wang and Mr. Li are neighbors. Read this passage about their families, then answer the questions. INTERPRETIVE

王先生是學生。他爸爸是律師，媽媽是英文老師。王先生的哥哥是醫生。李先生和他妹妹都是學生。李先生的爸爸和姐姐都是醫生，媽媽是老師。

1 If the two families vacation together, how many plane tickets should they book?

_____

2 How many doctors are there between the two families? Who are they?

_____

3 If Mr. Wang's mother were to have a colleague in the Li family, who would it most likely be?

_____

4 How many students are there between the two families?

_____

5 What does Mr. Li's father do? Is anyone from the Wang family in the same profession?

_____

B Read this dialogue, check the proper spaces on the form to indicate the professions of Little Gao's family members, then mark the statements true or false. INTERPRETIVE

小王：請問，你爸爸是律師嗎？

小高：不，他是老師。我家有兩個老師，兩個醫生，一個律師。

小王：你家有五口人嗎？

小高：不，我家有四口人。我和我媽媽都是醫生。我哥哥是老師，也是律師。

	Little Gao	Father	Mother	Older Brother
Lawyer				
Doctor				
Teacher				

1 _____ Little Wang seems to know Little Gao's family very well.

2 _____ Little Gao seems to have miscounted the people in his family.

3 _____ Little Gao's older brother is not only a teacher, but also a lawyer.

C Review this business card, then mark the statements true or false. INTERPRETIVE

韓 沐 新 律師　合夥人

律師事務所

地址：北京建國門外大街XX號賽特大廈XXXX室　　郵編：100004
電話：(8610) 6515 XXXX　　　　　　　直綫：(8610)6515 XXXX
手機：1390115 XXXX　　　　　　　　　傳真：(8610)6528 XXXX
E-mail: muxinh@ XXXX

1 _____ This person's family name is Li.

2 _____ This person is a doctor.

3 _____ This person works in Beijing.

Writing and Grammar Exercises

A Write the characters that include the radical for woman, 女, then provide each character's meaning in English.

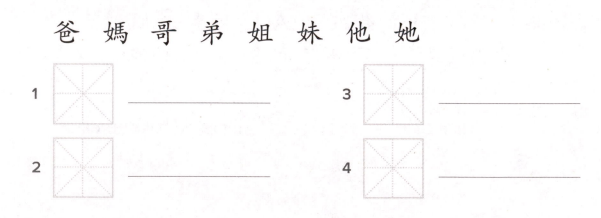

爸　媽　哥　弟　姐　妹　他　她

1 ☐ _____   **3** ☐ _____

2 ☐ _____   **4** ☐ _____

B Answer these questions about family in complete sentences, using 有 or 沒有. If your answer is affirmative, state how many siblings you have, following the example below. INTERPERSONAL

Q: 你有哥哥嗎？

A: 我有兩個哥哥。(affirmative)

A: 我沒有哥哥。(negative)

1 Q: 你有哥哥嗎？

A: _____

2 Q: 你有姐姐嗎？

A: _____

3 Q: 你有弟弟嗎？

A: _____

4 Q: 你有妹妹嗎？

A: _____

C Rewrite these sentences using 都, following the example below. PRESENTATIONAL

小高是學生，王朋也是學生。

小高和王朋都是學生。

1 高文中有姐姐，李友也有姐姐。

_____

2 那個男孩子姓李，那個女孩子也姓李。

_____

3 李友沒有我的照片，王朋也沒有我的照片。

_____

4 她哥哥不是律師，她弟弟也不是律師。

_____

5 這個人不叫白英愛，那個人也不叫白英愛。

_____

D Fill in the blanks with the appropriate question words: 什麼, 誰, 誰的, or 幾. PRESENTATIONAL

1 Q: 他妹妹叫_____名字？

A: 他妹妹叫高美美。

2 Q: 李老師家有_____口人？

A: 他家有三口人。

3 Q: 他爸爸做_____工作？

A: 他爸爸是醫生。

4 Q: 那個美國人是_____？

A: 他叫 Sam Freedman，是我的老師。

5 Q: 那是_____照片？

A: 那是白律師的照片。

Translate these sentences into Chinese. PRESENTATIONAL

1 Student A: How many people are there in Mr. Wang's family?

_____

Student B: There are five people in his family.

_____

2 Student A: What do his parents do?

_____

Student B: Both his mother and father are teachers.

_____

3 Student A: How many daughters does he have?

_____

Student B: He doesn't have any. He has three boys.

_____

4 Student A: My dad is a doctor. My mom is a lawyer. How about your mom and dad?

_____

Student B: My mom is a lawyer, too. My dad is a teacher.

_____

5 (Students A and B are looking at a picture on Student B's desk.)

Student A: Who is this?

_____

Student B: This is my older sister. Her name is Wang Xiaoying.

_____

Student A: What does she do?

_____

Student B: My sister and I both are college students. How many sisters do you have?

_____

Student A: I have an older sister, too. Here is a picture of her. She has a daughter.

_____

F Write about your family. PRESENTATIONAL

1 List your family members in Chinese.

_____

_____

2 State what each of your family members does. It's okay to write their occupations in *pinyin*.

_____

_____

_____

3 Prepare an oral presentation: Write a brief introduction of your family using the framework provided. Memorize the introduction and present your family to the class using a family portrait.

你好，我姓_____，叫_____。
我是____學生。這家有____口人，_____
_____和我。這是我家人的照片。這是我爸
爸，這是我媽媽，這個人是我_____……我
爸爸是_____，媽媽是_____，_____
是_____……

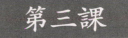

時間
Time and Date

 Check off the following items as you learn them.

Useful Expressions

[ ] When is your birthday?

[ ] I'll treat you to dinner.

[ ] Thank you very much!

[ ] What time is it now?

[ ] Goodbye!

Cultural Norms

[ ] Date formats

[ ] Calendar types

[ ] Birthday customs

[ ] Counting age

[ ] Auspicious numbers

As you progress through the lesson, note other useful expressions and cultural norms you would like to learn.

_____

_____

_____

Dialogue 1: Out for a Birthday Dinner

Listening Comprehension

A Listen to the Textbook Dialogue 1 audio, then mark these statements true or false. INTERPRETIVE

1 _____ Gao Wenzhong is eighteen years old this year.

2 _____ September 12 is Thursday.

3 _____ Bai Ying'ai will treat Gao Wenzhong to dinner on Thursday.

4 _____ Gao Wenzhong is American, but he likes Chinese food.

5 _____ Bai Ying'ai refuses to eat Chinese food.

6 _____ They will have dinner together at 6:30 p.m.

B Listen to the Workbook Dialogue 1 audio, then circle the most appropriate choice. INTERPRETIVE

1 What is today's date?

a May 10

b June 10

c October 5

d October 6

2 What day of the week is it today?

a Thursday

b Friday

c Saturday

d Sunday

3 What day of the week is October 7?

a Thursday

b Friday

c Saturday

d Sunday

C Listen to the Workbook Dialogue 2 audio, then circle the most appropriate choice. INTERPRETIVE

1 What time does the man propose to meet for the appointment?

a 6:30

b 7:00

c 7:30

d 8:00

2 What time do they finally agree upon?

    a 6:30

    b 7:00

    c 7:30

    d 8:00

3 On what day of the week are they going to meet?

    a Thursday

    b Friday

    c Saturday

    d Sunday

Pinyin and Tone

A Identify the characters with the same initials (*sh*, *s*, or *x*) and write them in *pinyin*.

歲　十　謝　誰　四　喜

1 *sh:* _____

2 *s:* _____

3 *x:* _____

B Compare the tones of these characters. Indicate the tones with 1 (first tone), 2 (second tone), 3 (third tone), 4 (fourth tone), or 0 (neutral tone).

1 號 _____ 好 _____

2 星 _____ 姓 _____

3 還 _____ 孩 _____

4 是 _____ 十 _____

Speaking

A Answer these questions in Chinese based on Textbook Dialogue 1. PRESENTATIONAL

1 When is Gao Wenzhong's birthday?

2 How old is Gao Wenzhong?

3 Who is going to treat whom?

4 What is Gao Wenzhong's nationality?

5 What kind of food are they going to have?

6 What time is the dinner?

B In pairs, role-play the following situation. Today is your partner's birthday. Find out how old he/she is and offer to take him/her out to dinner. Ask if he/she prefers Chinese or American food and decide when to eat. INTERPERSONAL

Reading Comprehension

A Based on the information on the sticky note, circle the most appropriate choice. INTERPRETIVE

九月十八日
星期四

1 What day of the week is September 15?
a Monday
b Tuesday
c Friday
d Sunday

2 What is the date of the following Thursday?
a September 22
b September 23
c September 24
d September 25

B Fill in the blanks in English based on the calendar. INTERPRETIVE

1 The date on this calendar is _____.

2 The day of the week is _____.

3 Next month is _____.

4 The day after tomorrow is a _____.

Circle the correct way to write "June 3, 2019" in Chinese. INTERPRETIVE

1 6月3號2019年

2 3號6月2019年

3 6月2019年3號

4 2019年6月3號

D Read this passage, then mark the statements true or false. INTERPRETIVE

　　這個星期六是十一月二號，是小王的媽媽的生日。小王請他媽媽吃飯。王媽媽很喜歡我，小王也請我吃飯。吃什麼呢？王媽媽是北京人，喜歡吃中國菜。我是紐約人，可是我也喜歡吃中國菜。

1 ____ Saturday is Little Wang's birthday.

2 ____ Little Wang's mother will take her son to dinner this Saturday.

3 ____ The speaker seems to know Little Wang's mother well.

4 ____ The speaker is American, and Little Wang's mother is Chinese.

5 ____ They will most likely have a Chinese dinner on Saturday.

E What are the dates for the exhibition advertised on this flyer, and on which university campus is it being held? INTERPRETIVE

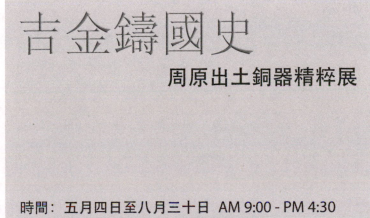

吉金鑄國史

周原出土銅器精粹展

時間：五月四日至八月三十日　AM 9:00 - PM 4:30
展出地點：紐英大學考古與藝術博物館

A Which of these characters are based on the left-right pattern and which on the top-bottom pattern? After filling in the answers, write the characters in the spaces provided.

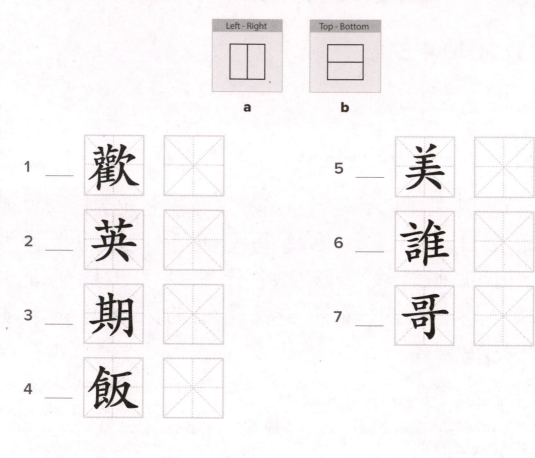

Left - Right

Top - Bottom

a

b

1 ___ 歡

2 ___ 英

3 ___ 期

4 ___ 飯

5 ___ 美

6 ___ 誰

7 ___ 哥

B Write these numbers in Chinese characters. PRESENTATIONAL

1 15 _____

2 93 _____

3 47 _____

4 62 _____

5 Your phone number _____

6 Your birthday _____ 月 _____ 號

C Write out the questions to which these statements are the appropriate answers. Use 還是 in each question, following the example below. PRESENTATIONAL

王朋

Q: 王朋是中國人還是美國人？

A: 王朋是中國人。

1 你

Q: _____ ?

A: 我喜歡吃美國菜。

2 李友的爸爸

Q: _____ ?

A: 他是律師。

3 高文中

Q: _____ ?

A: 高文中有姐姐。

D Rearrange these Chinese words into sentences, using the English sentences as clues. PRESENTATIONAL

1 我 ｜ 晚飯 ｜ 你 ｜ 怎麼樣 ｜ 吃 ｜ 請 ｜ 星期四

(I'll take you out to dinner on Thursday. How about it?)

_____

2 星期四 ｜ 星期五 ｜ 晚飯 ｜ 我 ｜ 你 ｜ 還是 ｜ 請 ｜ 吃

(Are you taking me out to dinner on Thursday or Friday?)

_____

3 哥哥｜小白｜喜歡｜他｜我｜我｜可是｜不｜喜歡

(I do not like Little Bai, but I like his older brother.)

_____

4 美國人｜美國菜｜可是｜他｜不｜喜歡｜吃｜是

(He is American, but he does not like eating American food.)

_____

E Answer these questions according to your own circumstances. INTERPERSONAL

1 Q: 你今年多大？

A: _____

2 Q: 你的生日（是）幾月幾號？

A: _____

3 Q: 你喜歡吃美國菜還是中國菜？

A: _____

F Translate these sentences into Chinese. PRESENTATIONAL

1 Student A: When is your birthday?

_____

  Student B: My birthday is September 30.

_____

2 Student A: What day of the week is September 30?

_____

Student B: September 30 is Friday.

_____

3 Student A: How old are you?

_____

Student B: I'm eighteen.

_____

4 Student A: How about I treat you to dinner on Thursday?

_____

Student B: Great! Thanks. See you Thursday.

_____

5 (Little Wang's girlfriend has never met Little Wang's parents. She is planning to invite them out to dinner, but wants to find out what they like to eat first.)

Little Wang: What time are we having dinner on Saturday night?

_____

Girlfriend: How about 7:30?

_____

Little Wang: Okay. Who are we inviting for dinner?

_____

Girlfriend: We'll invite your mom and dad.

_____

Little Wang: Great.

_____

Girlfriend: Do they like American or Chinese food?

_____

Little Wang: They like American, and they like Chinese, too.

_____

G Complete these tasks in Chinese. PRESENTATIONAL

1 Write down today's date.

_____

2 Write down the current time.

_____

3 Who's your idol/hero? Your idol/hero could be one of your family members or someone famous. If your idol/hero is someone famous, go online and find out his/her age, birthday, family members, and what cuisine he/she prefers. Write a personal profile of your idol/hero, and share it with your teacher/class.

_____

_____

_____

_____

_____

Dialogue 2: Dinner Invitation

Audio

Listening Comprehension

A Listen to the Textbook Dialogue 2 audio, then mark these statements true or false. INTERPRETIVE

1 _____ Wang Peng is not busy today.

2 _____ Wang Peng will be busy tomorrow.

3 _____ Bai Ying'ai is inviting Wang Peng to dinner.

4 _____ Tomorrow is Bai Ying'ai's birthday.

5 _____ Li You is Bai Ying'ai's schoolmate.

B Listen to the Workbook Dialogue 1 audio, then mark these statements true or false. INTERPRETIVE

1 _____ Both speakers in the dialogue are Chinese.

2 _____ The man invites the woman to dinner because it will be his birthday tomorrow.

3 _____ The man likes Chinese food.

4 _____ The woman only likes American food.

C Listen to the Workbook Dialogue 2 audio, then mark these statements true or false. INTERPRETIVE

1 _____ Today the woman is busy.

2 _____ Today the man is not busy.

3 _____ Tomorrow both the man and the woman will be busy.

Pinyin and Tone

A Identify the characters with the same initials (either *j* or *x*) and write them in *pinyin*.

現　京　星　喜　見

1 *j:* _____

2 *x:* _____

B Compare the tones of these characters. Indicate the tones with 1 (first tone), 2 (second tone), 3 (third tone), 4 (fourth tone), or 0 (neutral tone).

1 事 _____ 十 _____

2 人 _____ 認 _____

3 有 _____ 友 _____

Speaking

A Answer these questions in Chinese based on Textbook Dialogue 2. PRESENTATIONAL

1 Why does Bai Ying'ai ask if Wang Peng is busy tomorrow?

2 When is Wang Peng busy?

3 Who else will go to the dinner tomorrow?

4 Does Bai Ying'ai know Li You? How do you know?

B In pairs, ask for today's date, the day of the week, and the current time. INTERPERSONAL

C In pairs, role-play the following scenario. Your partner's sibling has a birthday coming up, and you would like to invite him/her to dinner. Find out when the sibling's birthday is, when he/she is available, and what type of cuisine he/she prefers. INTERPERSONAL

Reading Comprehension

A Rewrite these times in ordinary numeric notation (e.g., 1:00, 2:15, 3:30 p.m.). INTERPRETIVE

1 三點 _____

2 六點三刻 _____

3 晚上八點 _____

4 晚上九點一刻 _____

5 晚上十一點半 _____

B Read this dialogue, then mark the statements true or false. INTERPRETIVE

男：你好。今天我請你吃晚飯，怎麼樣？

女：是嗎？我不認識你，你為什麼請我吃飯？

男：因為今天是我的生日，可是沒有人請我吃飯……

女：先生，你為什麼不請你的朋友吃飯？

男：因為他們今天都很忙。

1 _____ The two people are friends.

2 _____ The man needs someone to celebrate his birthday with him.

3 _____ The woman accepts the man's invitation readily.

4 _____ The woman is the only one that the man invites to dinner.

5 _____ According to the man, his friends are too busy today to celebrate his birthday.

C Read this dialogue, then answer the questions by circling the most appropriate choice. INTERPRETIVE

小白：今天是幾月幾號？

小李：今天是二月二十八號。

小白：是嗎？明天是我的生日。我的生日是二月二十九號。明天晚上我請你吃晚飯，怎麼樣？

小李：太好了，謝謝。可是明天不是二月二十九號。

小白：那明天是幾月幾號？

小李：明天是三月一號。你今年沒有生日。

1 Which of these statements is true?

    a   Little Bai has been expecting her birthday all week.

    b   Little Bai almost forgot that her birthday was coming up.

    c   Little Li has been expecting Little Bai's birthday.

2 What will tomorrow's date be?

    a   February 28

    b   February 29

    c   March 1

3 Which of these statements is true?

    a   Little Bai has forgotten her birthday.

    b   Little Li gave the wrong date for tomorrow.

    c   Little Bai's birthday is off this year's calendar.

D Complete this application form to study abroad in China. The form asks for your name in Chinese. Invent one if you don't already have one. INTERPRETIVE

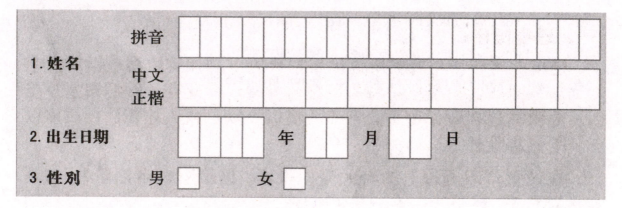

Writing and Grammar

A Write the common radical and the characters, then provide the characters' meanings. Consider their relationship with the radical.

期　明

B Rewrite these date and time phrases in Chinese characters. PRESENTATIONAL

1 November 12 _____

2 Friday evening _____

3 7:00 this evening _____

4 8:30 p.m. Saturday _____

5 a quarter after nine _____

C Complete these exchanges. PRESENTATIONAL

1 Q: 今天（是）幾月幾號？

   A: _____ 。

2 Q: 你的生日（是）_____ ？

   A: 我的生日（是）_____ 。

3 Q: 你今年多大？

   A: _____ 。

4 Q: 現在幾點？

   A: 現在 _____ 。

5 Q: _____ ？

   A: 我五點三刻吃晚飯。

D Write out the questions using "A-not-A" form, following the example below. PRESENTATIONAL

   Q: 王先生是不是北京人？

   A: 王先生是北京人。

1 Q: _____

   A: 小李沒有弟弟。

2 Q: _____

   A: 小王不喜歡吃美國菜。

3 Q: _____

   A: 小高的姐姐工作。

4 Q: _____

   A: 高律師明天很忙。

E Based on Textbook Dialogue 2, answer these questions with 因為. INTERPERSONAL

1 白英愛為什麼請高文中吃飯？

   _____

2 白英愛為什麼問 (to ask) 王朋忙不忙？

   _____

3 王朋為什麼認識李友？

   _____

F Rewrite these sentences using 還, following the example below. PRESENTATIONAL

   我有一個哥哥。我有一個弟弟。

   我有一個哥哥，還有一個弟弟。

1 她喜歡吃中國菜。她喜歡吃美國菜。

   _____

2 他認識王朋。他認識李友。

3 白英愛有她哥哥的照片。白英愛有她妹妹的
   照片。

   _____

1 **Student A:** What time is it right now?

   _____

   Student B: It's 8:45.

   _____

2 **Student A:** Are you busy or not this evening?

   _____

   Student B: I have things to do this evening, but am available tomorrow evening.

   _____

3 **Student A:** Does your brother have a girlfriend or not?

   _____

   Student B: He doesn't.

   _____

   Student A: Great! I'd like to invite him to dinner on Friday.

   _____

   Student B: He's busy on Friday, but I am free.

   _____

   Student A: Really? But I like your brother, not you.

   _____

H Write a birthday party invitation card in Chinese. Make sure to mention the date, the day of the week, the time, the food you will serve, and that you will be hosting at home. PRESENTATIONAL

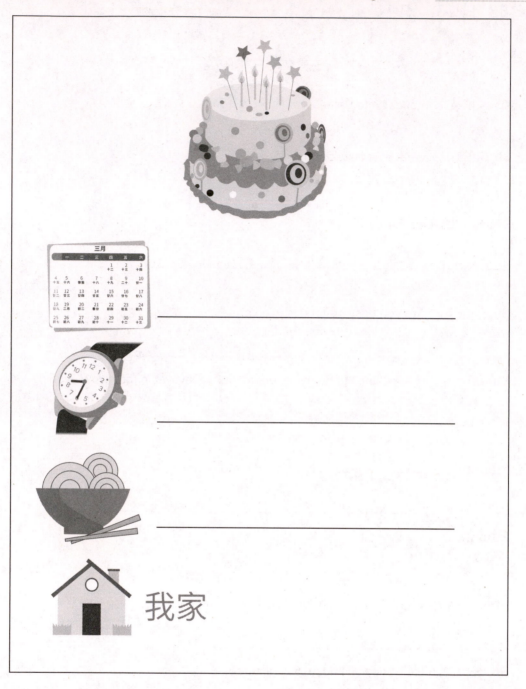

我家

_____

_____

_____

I Write a note to your friend inviting him/her to have dinner with you tomorrow to celebrate your birthday. PRESENTATIONAL

_____

_____

_____

Lesson 4

第四課

愛 好
Hobbies

 Check off the following items as you learn them.

Useful Expressions

[ ] Long time no see.

[ ] How are you?

[ ] What do you like to do on weekends?

[ ] I like watching movies.

[ ] Really? Great!

Cultural Norms

[ ] Diminutives

[ ] Restaurant etiquette

[ ] Popular pastimes

As you progress through the lesson, note other useful expressions and cultural norms you would like to learn.

_____

_____

_____

Dialogue 1: Discussing Hobbies

🔊 **Audio**

Listening Comprehension

A Listen to the Textbook Dialogue 1 audio, then mark these statements true or false. INTERPRETIVE

1 _____ Gao Wenzhong likes music.

2 _____ Bai Ying'ai reads a lot every weekend.

3 _____ Bai Ying'ai likes to sing and dance on weekends.

4 _____ Both Gao Wenzhong and Bai Ying'ai seem to like going to the movies.

5 _____ Gao Wenzhong is inviting Bai Ying'ai to dinner and a movie tonight.

6 _____ Gao Wenzhong and Bai Ying'ai will be joined by two friends.

B Listen to the Workbook Dialogue 1 audio, then circle the most appropriate choice. INTERPRETIVE

1 What does the man like to do most?

a listen to music

b play ball

c go to the movies

d go dancing

2 If the man and the woman decide to do something together, where are they most likely to go?

a a movie

b a concert

c a dance

d a ball game

C Listen to the Workbook Dialogue 2 audio, then circle the most appropriate choice. INTERPRETIVE

1 What does the man invite the woman to?

a dinner

b a movie

c a dance

d a concert

2 Why does the man ask the woman out?

a She invited him to dinner previously.

b She likes watching movies.

c Tomorrow is his birthday.

d He has a lot of free time.

3 Which of these statements is true?

   a   The woman doesn't accept the invitation although she isn't busy tomorrow.

   b   The woman doesn't accept the invitation because she'll be busy tomorrow.

   c   The woman accepts the invitation although she'll be busy tomorrow.

   d   The woman accepts the invitation because she isn't busy tomorrow.

Pinyin and Tone

A Identify the characters with the same initials (either *d* or *t*) and write them in *pinyin*.

對　電　跳　聽　打　天

1 *d:* _____

2 *t:* _____

B Compare the tones of these characters. Indicate the tones with 1 (first tone), 2 (second tone), 3 (third tone), 4 (fourth tone), or 0 (neutral tone).

1 打 _____ 大 _____   **4** 歌 _____ 哥 _____

2 電 _____ 點 _____   **5** 舞 _____ 五 _____

3 視 _____ 是 _____   **6** 唱 _____ 常 _____

Speaking

A Answer these questions in Chinese based on Textbook Dialogue 1. PRESENTATIONAL

1 What does Gao Wenzhong like to do on weekends?

2 What does Bai Ying'ai like to do on weekends?

3 What will Bai Ying'ai and Gao Wenzhong do this evening?

4 Who is treating this evening?

5 Who else might also go this evening?

B Discuss your interests and hobbies with your friends, then invite them to an event on social media based on your common interests. INTERPERSONAL

Reading Comprehension

A Draw a line connecting each image with the phrase it represents. INTERPRETIVE

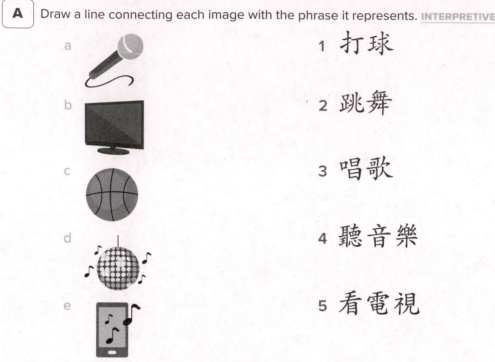

a

b

c

d

e

1 打球

2 跳舞

3 唱歌

4 聽音樂

5 看電視

B Read this paragraph, then indicate Little Gao's activities on the day planner in English. Note the activities, what time they will occur, and the people who are coming. INTERPRETIVE

這個星期小高晚上都很忙。今天星期一，晚上八點小高請朋友跳舞，明天晚上六點半請同學吃飯，星期三晚上九點一刻請女朋友看電影，星期四晚上打球，星期五晚上唱歌。那週末他做什麼呢？看書嗎？不對！小高不喜歡看書，週末那兩天他看電視，看電視，看電視……

Monday	Tuesday	Wednesday	Thursday	Friday	Saturday	Sunday

C Read this passage, then answer the questions in English. INTERPRETIVE

　　我大哥認識一個女孩子，她的名字叫李明英。李小姐今年二十歲，是大學生。我大哥很喜歡她，常常請她吃晚飯。週末兩個人喜歡去跳舞、看電影。可是李小姐的爸爸和媽媽不喜歡我大哥，因為他今年三十八歲，可是沒有工作。我也不喜歡他們兩個人做男女朋友，因為李小姐是我的同學。

1　What three things do we know about Miss Li?

_____

2　What do Miss Li and the narrator's older brother like to do on weekends?

_____

3　What are the two reasons that Miss Li's parents don't like their daughter dating the narrator's older brother?

_____

4　What's the narrator's attitude toward the relationship? Why does she feel this way?

_____

D What listings are referred to in this newspaper clipping? What dates were the listings good for?
INTERPRETIVE

電視電影節目表
7月13日(星期二)——7月14日(星期三)

Writing and Grammar

A Write the characters from the group below that are formed with the top-bottom pattern, then provide each character's meaning (consult a dictionary if needed).

週　音　做　作　客　那　常　是

1 ☐ _____   3 ☐ _____

2 ☐ _____   4 ☐ _____

B In the blanks, report on what these four characters like and don't like to do. PRESENTATIONAL

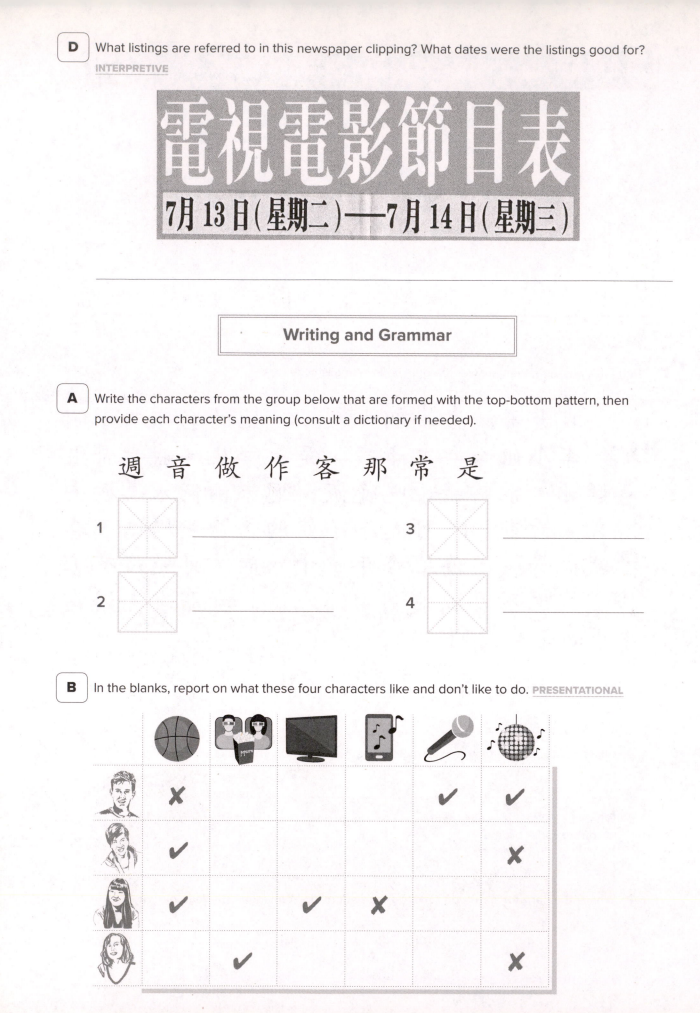

1 _____

2 _____

3 _____

4 _____

C Use a word or phrase from each of these four groups to make four sentences based on Chinese word order: subject + time + verb + object. PRESENTATIONAL

美國菜，球，音樂，電影

明天晚上，這個週末，星期四，今天

去看，去聽，去打，去吃

我們，我爸爸媽媽，小白和小高，王朋和李友

1 _____

2 _____

3 _____

4 _____

D Translate these sentences into Chinese. PRESENTATIONAL

1 Q: Do you often see movies on weekends?

_____

A: I am busy on weekends. I work.

_____

2 Q: I'll take you dancing tonight. How about it?

_____

A: Thanks. But I don't like dancing.

_____

3 Q: What do you like to do?

_____

A: Sometimes I like to read. Sometimes I also like listening to music.

_____

4 Q: Why is it your treat today?

_____

A: Because it was your treat yesterday. It's my treat today.

_____

5 Q: You like watching foreign films, right?

_____

A: That's correct. I often watch foreign films.

_____

E Fill in the blanks according to your circumstances. PRESENTATIONAL

我姓_____，叫_____，是_____學生。我家有_____口人，_____和我。我爸爸是_____，媽媽是_____。

我喜歡_____，有的時候也喜歡_____，可是我不喜歡_____。我週末_____忙，常常_____。

Dialogue 2: Let's Play Ball

| Listening Comprehension |

A Listen to the Textbook Dialogue 2 audio, then mark these statements true or false. INTERPRETIVE

1 ____ Gao Wenzhong does not like playing ball.

2 ____ Wang Peng wants to play ball this weekend.

3 ____ Gao Wenzhong is very interested in watching a ball game.

4 ____ Wang Peng is going out to eat with Gao Wenzhong.

5 ____ Gao Wenzhong likes to sleep.

6 ____ In the end, Wang Peng gives up on the idea of going out with Gao Wenzhong.

B Listen to the Workbook Dialogue 1 audio, then mark these statements true or false. INTERPRETIVE

1 ____ The woman doesn't like Chinese movies because her Chinese isn't good enough.

2 ____ The woman prefers American movies over Chinese movies.

3 ____ The man agrees that American movies are more interesting.

C Listen to the Workbook Dialogue 2 audio, then mark these statements true or false. INTERPRETIVE

1 ____ The woman invites the man to a concert.

2 ____ The man wants to play ball.

3 ____ The man invites the woman to go dancing.

D Listen to the Workbook Narrative audio, then circle the most appropriate choice. INTERPRETIVE

1 Where does the speaker spend most of his spare time?

   a at movie theaters

   b at concert halls

   c in front of the TV

   d at the library

2 What does Wang Peng like?

   a movies and TV

   b dancing and reading

   c dancing and music

   d only books

3 Which of these statements about the speaker and Wang Peng is true?

    a Wang Peng likes to read.

    b The speaker likes to watch TV.

    c Both the speaker and Wang Peng like to dance.

    d Wang Peng and the speaker are classmates.

Pinyin and Tone

A Identify the characters with the same finals (either *ie* or *iu*) and write them in *pinyin*.

别 謝 久 姐 紐 球

1 *ie:* _____

2 *iu:* _____

B Compare the tones of these characters. Indicate the tones with 1 (first tone), 2 (second tone), 3 (third tone), 4 (fourth tone), or 0 (neutral tone).

1 九 _____ 久 _____

2 思 _____ 四 _____

3 睡 _____ 水 _____

Speaking

A Answer these questions in Chinese based on Textbook Dialogue 2. PRESENTATIONAL

1 How does Wang Peng greet Gao Wenzhong?

2 Does Gao Wenzhong want to play ball? Why?

3 Does Gao Wenzhong want to go to the movies? Why?

4 What does Gao Wenzhong like to do?

5 What did Wang Peng finally decide to do this weekend?

B In pairs, role-play a conversation. Your partner is inviting you to do something. Keep rejecting your partner's suggestions and give reasons why you do not like those activities. INTERPERSONAL

A Match the questions on the left with the appropriate replies on the right. INTERPRETIVE

1 _____ 你叫什麼名字？   a 我明天不忙。

2 _____ 這是你弟弟嗎？   b 今天晚上我很忙。

3 _____ 你明天忙不忙？   c 我想看一個外國電影。

4 _____ 你認識小高嗎？   d 不，這是我哥哥。

5 _____ 你喜歡聽音樂嗎？   e 因為我喜歡吃美國菜。

6 _____ 你為什麼請我看電影？   f 認識，他是我同學。

7 _____ 我們為什麼不吃中國菜？   g 我叫王朋。

8 _____ 我們去打球，好嗎？   h 我覺得聽音樂沒有意思。

9 _____ 這個週末你做什麼？   i 我不想打球。

10 _____ 今天晚上我去找你，好嗎？ j 因為今天是你的生日。

Read this passage, then answer the questions by circling the most appropriate choice. INTERPRETIVE

小王和小李是同學。小王是英國人，他喜歡打球、看電視和看書。小李是美國人，她喜歡聽音樂、唱歌和跳舞。他們都喜歡看電影，可是小王只喜歡看美國電影，小李覺得美國電影沒有意思，只喜歡看外國電影。她覺得中國電影很有意思。

1　What activities does Little Wang enjoy?
　　a　watching TV and listening to music
　　b　watching Chinese movies and dancing
　　c　watching American movies and singing
　　d　playing ball and reading

2　What does Little Li like to do?
　　a　watching TV and listening to music
　　b　watching Chinese movies and dancing
　　c　watching American movies and dancing
　　d　playing ball and reading

3　Which of the following statements is true?
　　a　Little Wang and Little Li both like to watch TV.
　　b　Little Wang is American and he likes American movies.
　　c　Little Li is Chinese but she likes American movies.
　　d　Little Wang and Little Li go to the same school.

4　If Little Wang and Little Li want to do something they are both interested in, where can they go?
　　a　to a ball game
　　b　to a library
　　c　to a dance party
　　d　none of the above

C　Read this dialogue, then mark the statements true or false. INTERPRETIVE

小王：你喜歡看美國電影還是外國電影？

老李：我不喜歡看美國電影，也不喜歡看外國電影。

小王：你覺得中國音樂有意思還是美國音樂有意思？

老李：我覺得中國音樂和美國音樂都沒有意思。

小王：你常常看中文書還是英文書？

老李：我不看中文書，也不看英文書。

小王：那你喜歡吃中國菜還是美國菜？

老李：中國菜和美國菜我都喜歡吃。

1 ___ This conversation most likely takes place in the United States.

2 ___ Old Li likes European movies, not American movies.

3 ___ Old Li feels that both Chinese music and American music are boring.

4 ___ When Old Li reads, the book must be in a language other than English or Chinese.

5 ___ It seems Old Li does not like anything American or Chinese.

D Read this passage, then answer the questions in English. INTERPRETIVE

　　小李很喜歡打球，可是他的女朋友小文覺得打球沒有意思，她只喜歡看電影。明天是星期六，也是小文的生日。小李和小文想去看電影。可是看什麼電影呢？小李覺得 «The Benchwarmers» 這個電影有很多人打球，很有意思。小文不喜歡打球，可是也想去看那個電影。小李和小文都很高興，他們明天下午三點半去看電影。

1 What does Little Li like to do?

_____

2 Why does Little Li want to see a movie with Little Wen tomorrow?

_____

3 What makes the movie *The Benchwarmers* special to Little Li?

_____

4 Why are both Little Li and Little Wen happy?

_____

E Locate the channels for movies and music, respectively, on this Chinese TV guide. **INTERPRETIVE**

今明電視節目安排

8月 1日 週一電視

第一電視臺－1(綜合頻道)

19:55 電視劇：冼星海(5、6)
21:40 紀實十分

第二電視臺－2(經濟頻道)

20:25 經濟與法
21:30 經濟半小時

第三電視臺－3(綜藝頻道)

18:30 綜藝快報
19:05 動物世界
21:15 快樂驛站

第四電視臺－4(國際頻道)

20:10 走遍中國
20:40 海峽兩岸
21:00 中國新聞
21:30 今日關注
22:00 中國文藝

第五電視臺－5(體育頻道)

18:55 巔峰時刻
21:30 體育世界

第六電視臺－6(電影頻道)

21:48 世界電影之旅之資訊快車

第八電視臺－8(電視劇頻道)

19:30 電視劇：國家機密(15－17)

第十電視臺－10(科教頻道)

20:10 歷程
20:30 走進科學
20:40 講述

第十二電視臺－12(社會與法頻道)

20:00 大家看法
23:10 心靈訪談
23:30 電視劇：公安局長(7、8)

第十三電視臺－新聞頻道

20:30 新聞會客廳
21:30 國際觀察
21:55 天氣資訊

第十四電視臺－少兒頻道

19:00 中國動畫(精品版)
19:30 智慧樹
20:00 動漫世界

第十五電視臺－音樂頻道

20:10 經典

A Identify the patterns of 我 and 找, then write the characters that share the same pattern from the group below.

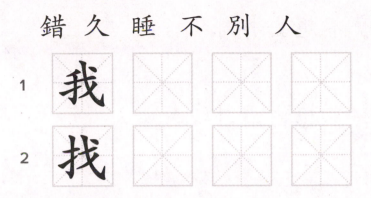

錯 久 睡 不 別 人

1 我

2 找

B Rearrange these Chinese words into sentences, using the English sentences as clues. PRESENTATIONAL

1 覺得 | 這個 | 沒有 | 電影 | 有 | 意思 | 你

(Do you think this movie is interesting?)

_____

2 王朋 | 去 | 週末 | 和 | 李友 | 這個 | 打球

(Wang Peng and Li You will go play ball this weekend.)

_____

3 今天晚上 | 他 | 看 | 電視 | 想 | 不 | 聽 |
音樂 | 想

(Tonight he wants to watch TV, not listen to music.)

_____

Based on Textbook Dialogue 2, answer these questions using 因為⋯所以⋯. INTERPERSONAL

1 Q: 高文中為什麼請白英愛看電影？

A: _____

2 Q: 高文中為什麼不想去打球？

A: _____

3 Q: 高文中為什麼不想去看球？

A: _____

D Answer these questions according to your own circumstances. INTERPERSONAL

1 Q: 你週末常常做什麼？

A: _____

2 Q: 你喜歡看美國電影還是外國電影？

A: _____

3 Q: 你今天晚上想幾點睡覺？

A: _____

4 Q: 你覺得打球有意思還是跳舞有意思？

A: _____

E Translate these sentences into Chinese. PRESENTATIONAL

1 Student A: Little Wang, long time no see. Are you busy?

_____

Student B: Long time no see, Little Gao. I've been busy. How about you?

_____

Student A: I'm busy, too.

2 **Student A:**   Let's go dancing this weekend, OK?

_____

Student B: I don't want to go. I only want to get some sleep.

_____

3 **Student A:**   I'd like to take you to see a foreign film.

_____

Student B: Thank you. But I think foreign films are boring.

_____

Student A: Never mind. I'll go find someone else.

_____

4 **Student A:**   What would you like to do tonight? How about watching TV?

_____

Student B: I think watching TV is boring. I like singing and dancing. I'd like to go singing tonight.

_____

Student A: OK.

_____

5 **Student A:**   Today is my birthday. I am nineteen years old. My friends will take me out for dinner and dancing tonight.

_____

Student B: You like dancing, right?

_____

Student A: Right, I like dancing. I often dance on weekends. How about you?

_____

Student B: I think dancing is boring.

_____

Student A: Is that so?!

_____

F   Based on the chart, report on Little Wang's plans for next week. PRESENTATIONAL

Monday	Tuesday	Wednesday	Thursday	Friday	Saturday	Sunday

_____

_____

_____

看朋友
Visiting Friends

 Check off the following items as you learn them.

Useful Expressions

[ ] Who is it?

[ ] Please come in!

[ ] Let me introduce you to each other.

[ ] Pleased to meet you!

[ ] I'm sorry.

Cultural Norms

[ ] Visiting etiquette

[ ] Standard greetings

[ ] Classification of tea

[ ] Popular beverages

As you progress through the lesson, note other useful expressions and cultural norms you would like to learn.

_____

_____

_____

Dialogue: Visiting a Friend's Place

🔊
Audio

Listening Comprehension

A Listen to the Textbook Dialogue audio, then mark these statements true or false. INTERPRETIVE

1 _____ Wang Peng and Li You had met Gao Wenzhong's older sister before.

2 _____ Li You was very happy to meet Gao Wenzhong's sister.

3 _____ Gao Wenzhong's sister is a student.

4 _____ Li You likes to drink tea.

5 _____ Gao Wenzhong's sister gave Li You a cola.

B Listen to the Workbook Dialogue 1 audio, then mark these statements true or false. INTERPRETIVE

1 _____ The man and the woman are speaking on the phone.

2 _____ The man and the woman have never met each other before.

3 _____ The man is looking for his younger brother.

C Listen to the Workbook Dialogue 2 audio, then circle the most appropriate choice. INTERPRETIVE

1 The dialogue most likely takes place between

  a two strangers.

  b a parent and a child.

  c two friends.

  d a teacher and a student.

2 Which of these statements about the woman is true?

  a She doesn't like TV in general but she likes what is on TV tonight.

  b She doesn't like TV in general and she likes what is on TV tonight even less.

  c She likes TV in general but she doesn't like what is on TV tonight.

  d She likes TV in general and she particularly likes what is on TV tonight.

3 What will they most likely end up doing?

  a watching TV

  b seeing a Chinese movie

  c reading an American novel

  d listening to Chinese music

Listen to the Workbook Dialogue 3 audio, then circle the most appropriate choice. INTERPRETIVE

1 Which of the following is the correct order of the woman's preferences?

a coffee, tea

b cola, coffee

c coffee, cola

d tea, coffee

2 Which beverage does the man not have?

a tea

b water

c cola

d coffee

3 Which beverage does the woman finally get?

a tea

b water

c cola

d coffee

Pinyin and Tone

A Identify the characters with the same initials (either *j* or *z*) and write them in *pinyin*.

進　在　子　介　坐　見

1 *j:* _____

2 *z:* _____

B Compare the tones of these characters. Indicate the tones with 1 (first tone), 2 (second tone), 3 (third tone), 4 (fourth tone), or 0 (neutral tone).

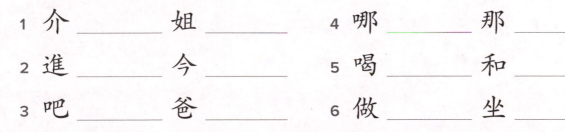

1 介 _____ 姐 _____   **4** 哪 _____ 那 _____

2 進 _____ 今 _____   **5** 喝 _____ 和 _____

3 吧 _____ 爸 _____   **6** 做 _____ 坐 _____

Speaking

A Answer these questions in Chinese based on the Textbook Dialogue. PRESENTATIONAL

1 Who went to Gao Wenzhong's house?

2 Had Wang Peng and Li You met Gao Wenzhong's sister before?

3 What is Gao Wenzhong's older sister's name?

4 How is Gao Wenzhong's house?

5 Where does Gao Wenzhong's older sister work?

6 What did Wang Peng want to drink?

7 Why did Li You ask for a glass of water?

B In pairs, role-play meeting someone for the first time. Exchange basic greetings, ask the other person his/her name, profession (or if he/she is a student), and hobbies. INTERPERSONAL

C In pairs, role-play visiting a friend's home. Compliment your friend's house. Your friend offers you coffee or tea, but you just want a glass of water. INTERPERSONAL

Reading Comprehension

A Read this description, then match the people with their preferred beverages. INTERPRETIVE

小高、小白和小王都是同學。小高不喜歡喝咖啡，也不喜歡喝茶。小白不喝可樂，也不常喝咖啡。小王只喜歡喝咖啡。

1 ____ Little Gao   a tea

2 ____ Little Bai   b coffee

3 ____ Little Wang   c cola

Read this dialogue, then mark the statements true or false. INTERPRETIVE

（王中去他的同學李文家玩兒。）

李文：王中，你想喝點兒什麼？

王中：給我一瓶可樂吧。

李文：對不起，我家沒有可樂。

王中：那給我一杯茶，好嗎？

李文：對不起，也沒有茶。

王中：那我喝一杯咖啡吧。

李文：對不起，我只有水。

王中：你家很大，也很漂亮，可是……

1 _____ Wang Zhong is visiting Li Wen's home.

2 _____ Wang Zhong seems to like tea better than water.

3 _____ Li Wen's refrigerator is full of all kinds of beverages.

4 _____ Wang Zhong is impressed by the beverages that Li Wen has offered.

C You have ninety Taiwan dollars. What three beverages can you order from this menu? INTERPRETIVE

1 _____

2 _____

3 _____

飲料

可樂/雪碧/健怡可樂........	M $25 L $30
柳橙汁...........................	M $35
鮮榨柳橙汁.....................	M $50
摩斯礦泉水.....................	M $18
冰咖啡/冰紅茶.................	M $30 L $35
熱咖啡/熱紅茶.................	M $30
奇異蔬果汁.....................	M $50
可可亞 (季節限定)............	M $30
咖啡歐蕾 (季節限定)........	M $30

Writing and Grammar

A Each of these characters shares the same radical, 口. Write the *pinyin* for the characters in the top row, compare them with the *pinyin* of the characters below, then consider the relationship between each pair.

1 呀 _____   2 哪 _____   3 啡 _____   4 吧 _____

牙 (yá)   那 (nà)   非 (fēi)   巴 (bā)

B Describe the images by writing the appropriate numbers, measure words, and nouns. PRESENTATIONAL

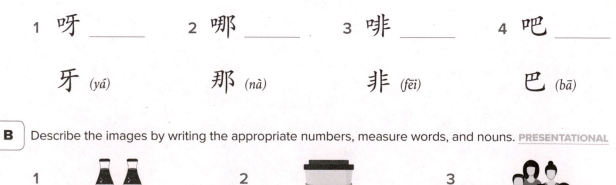

1   2   3

_____   _____   _____

C Rearrange these Chinese words into sentences, using the English sentences as clues. PRESENTATIONAL

1 常常 ｜ 王老師 ｜ 在學校 ｜ 看書

(Professor Wang often reads at school.)

_____

2 看電視 ｜ 週末 ｜ 我的同學 ｜ 在家

(My classmate watches TV at home on weekends.)

_____

3 小白 ｜ 工作 ｜ 星期五 ｜ 在哪兒

(Where does Little Bai work on Fridays?)

_____

D Answer these questions affirmatively and negatively, then circle the response that is true for you personally. PRESENTATIONAL

1 你的老師高不高？

Affirmative: _____

Negative: _____

2 你的醫生好不好？

Affirmative: _____

Negative: _____

3 你的英文書有沒有意思？

Affirmative: _____

Negative: _____

4 你今天高興不高興？

Affirmative: _____

Negative: _____

5 你家大嗎？

Affirmative: _____

Negative: _____

6 你們的學校漂亮嗎？

Affirmative: _____

Negative: _____

E The following is part of a conversation between Little Li, a waiter, and Mr. Gao, a customer. Complete the conversation by inserting the correct phrases or sentences listed below.

PRESENTATIONAL

1 您要英國茶還是
中國茶

2 可以，可以

3 好久不見

4 請坐，請坐

5 高先生

6 請進，請進

7 您想喝點什麼

Little Li: _____，_____。

Mr Gao: 小李，好久不見。

Little Li: _____。

Mr Gao: 好，謝謝。

Little Li: _____。

Mr. Gao: 我不想坐這兒，我想坐那兒。可以嗎？

Little Li: _____。

Little Li: _____ ?

Mr. Gao: 我想喝茶。

Little Li: _____ ?

Mr. Gao: 給我一杯英國茶吧!

F Translate these exchanges into Chinese. PRESENTATIONAL

1 Student A: Let me introduce you to each other. This is my classmate, Li Ming.

_____

_____

Student B: Mr. Li, my name is Wang Ying. Pleased to meet you.

_____

_____

Student C: Miss Wang, very pleased to meet you, too.

_____

2 Student A: Where do you work?

_____

Student B: I work at a school.

_____

3 Student A: What would you like to do this weekend? See a movie or go dancing?

_____

Student B: Let's go dancing!

_____

4 Student A: Would you like to have something to drink? Coffee or tea?

_____

Student B: I'll have a cup of coffee.

_____

G   You write an etiquette blog for tourists traveling to China. List five need-to-know expressions for hosts and guests. PRESENTATIONAL

Welcoming Host   **Gracious Guest**

_____   _____

_____   _____

_____   _____

_____   _____

_____   _____

Narrative: At a Friend's Place

Listening Comprehension

A Listen to the Textbook Narrative audio, then mark these statements true or false. **INTERPRETIVE**

1 _____ Gao Wenzhong's older sister works in a library.

2 _____ Wang Peng had two glasses of water at Wenzhong's house.

3 _____ Li You did not drink tea at Wenzhong's house.

4 _____ Wang Peng and Li You chatted and watched TV at Wenzhong's house.

5 _____ Wang Peng and Li You left Wenzhong's house at noon.

B Listen to the Workbook Narrative audio, then mark these statements true or false. **INTERPRETIVE**

1 _____ The speaker thinks that Little Bai and Little Li are old friends.

2 _____ The three people are most likely at the speaker's place.

3 _____ Little Bai told Little Li that he works in the library.

C Listen to the Workbook Dialogue audio, then circle the most appropriate choice. **INTERPRETIVE**

1 Where were little Bai and his younger brother Saturday night?

   a at home

   b at Little Gao's place

   c at Little Li's place

   d at Little Bai's brother's place

2 What did Little Bai's brother do at the party?

   a He had tea.

   b He watched TV.

   c He chatted with friends.

   d He danced.

3 How did Little Bai spend most of the evening?

   a drinking tea and watching TV

   b chatting and watching TV

   c drinking tea and chatting

   d drinking tea, chatting, and watching TV

Pinyin and Tone

A Identify the characters with the same finals (either *uan* or *iao*) and write them in *pinyin*.

歡 算 聊 館 跳 叫

1 *iao:* _____

2 *uan:* _____

B Compare the tones of these characters. Indicate the tones with 1 (first tone), 2 (second tone), 3 (third tone), 4 (fourth tone), or 0 (neutral tone).

1 玩 _____ 晚 _____   2 了 _____ 樂 _____

Speaking

A Answer these questions in Chinese based on the Textbook Narrative. PRESENTATIONAL

1 Why did Wang Peng and Li You go to Gao Wenzhong's house?

2 Where does Gao Wenzhong's sister work?

3 What did Wang Peng drink? How much?

4 What did Wang Peng and Li You do at Gao Wenzhong's house?

5 When did Wang Peng and Li You go home?

B In pairs, ask each other what beverage you had last night, how much, and what else you did. Then present the information you've gathered. INTERPERSONAL & PRESENTATIONAL

A Read this note, then answer the questions in English. INTERPRETIVE

小張：

　　明天晚上七點半學校有一個中國電影，我們一起去看，好嗎？我明天晚上來找你。

小高
十月五日晚上九點半

1　Who wrote the note?

_____

2　What time is the movie?

_____

3　Where is the movie?

_____

4　When will the two friends meet?

_____

5　When was the note written?

_____

昨天是小李的生日，小李請了小高、小張和王朋三個同學去她家吃飯。他們七點吃晚飯。小李的家不大，可是很漂亮。小李的爸爸是老師，他很有意思。小李的媽媽是醫生，昨天很忙，九點才回家吃晚飯。小李的哥哥和姐姐都不在家吃飯。王朋和小李的爸爸媽媽一起喝茶、聊天。小高、小張和小李一起喝可樂、看電視。小高、小張和王朋十一點才回家。

1 _____ Little Li's home is both large and beautiful.

2 _____ Little Li celebrated her birthday with her classmates but not with her entire family.

3 _____ Wang Peng drank cola with his friends.

4 _____ Little Li's friends left her home about the same time.

C Based on the passage in (B), circle the most appropriate choice.

1 **Who was late for dinner last night?**
   a Little Gao
   b Little Zhang
   c Little Li's father
   d Little Li's mother

2 **Which of the following statements is true?**
   a Little Li's mother is a teacher.
   b Little Li's father is an interesting person.
   c Little Li's brother and sister were home last night.
   d Wang Peng talked with Little Li all evening.

Read this passage, then mark the statements true or false. **INTERPRETIVE**

今天小高去找他的同學小王，小王的妹妹也在家。可是小高不認識小王的妹妹。小王介紹了一下。小王的妹妹也是他們學校的學生。她很漂亮，喜歡唱歌和看書。這個週末小高想請小王的妹妹去喝咖啡、看電影。

1 _____ Little Gao has met Little Wang's sister before.

2 _____ Little Gao and Little Wang's sister attend the same school.

3 _____ Little Gao's sister likes to dance.

4 _____ Little Gao would like to invite Little Wang and his sister to see a movie this weekend.

Writing and Grammar

A Which of these characters are based on the left-right pattern, and which on the enclosing pattern? After filling in the answers, write the characters in the spaces provided.

a   b

1 ___ 玩

2 ___ 瓶

3 ___ 國

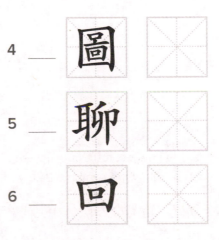

4 ___ 圖

5 ___ 聊

6 ___ 回

B This chart shows what Little Gao did and didn't do last night. Write questions-and-answers based on the information provided, following the example below. PRESENTATIONAL

Q: 他昨天晚上打球了嗎？

A: 他昨天晚上沒打球。

1 Q: _____

   A: _____

2 Q: _____

   A: _____

3 Q: _____

   A: _____

4 Q: _____

   A: _____

5 Q: _____

   A: _____

C Based on the images, form questions-and-answers about the beverages Little Wang drank at the party. Follow the example below. PRESENTATIONAL

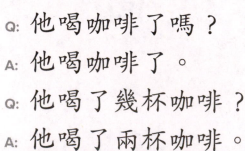

Q: 他喝咖啡了嗎？

A: 他喝咖啡了。

Q: 他喝了幾杯咖啡？

A: 他喝了兩杯咖啡。

1 Q: _____

    A: _____

    Q: _____

    A: _____

2 Q: _____

    A: _____

    Q: _____

    A: _____

3 Q: _____

    A: _____

    Q: _____

    A: _____

D | Little Li is always late. Summarize what her friends have told you about her habits, following the example below. PRESENTATIONAL

6:00 p.m.　　吃晚飯　　6:30 p.m.

我們六點吃晚飯，她六點半才來。

1　7:30 p.m.　　看電影　　7:45 p.m.

_____

2　8:00 a.m.　　工作　　8:15 a.m.

_____

3　6:30 p.m.　　打球　　7:00 p.m.

_____

1 Q: Did you play ball last night?

_____

A: No, I didn't. I was too busy.

_____

2 Q: Did you have coffee?

_____

A: I didn't. I only drank two glasses of water.

_____

3 Q: Why didn't you go to bed until 12:00 a.m.?

_____

A: Because I saw two movies, and didn't go home until 11:30 p.m.

_____

_____

4 I first met Gao Wenzhong at the library. He is tall and from England. He likes to chat. We often chat and have tea together. He thinks dancing is fun. I will take him dancing tonight.

_____

_____

_____

F Describe a recent visit to a friend's place. Mention what you did and what beverages you had.
PRESENTATIONAL

Bringing It Together (Lessons 1–5)

> **Pinyin and Tone**

A Compare the characters' pronunciation and tones, then write them in *pinyin*.

1 你們 _____   你好 _____

2 不錯 _____   不來 _____

3 音樂 _____   可樂 _____

4 覺得 _____   睡覺 _____

> **Radicals**

A Group these characters according to their radicals.

喝　館　孩　打　晚　星　紹　快　說　找
今　時　國　他　圖　睡　吃　杯　學　妹
呢　們　忙　誰　姓　看　給　樣　飯　回

Radical   **Characters**

1 _____   _____

2 _____   _____

3 _____   _____

4 _____   _____

5 _____   _____

6 _____   _____

7 _____

8 _____

9 _____

10 _____

11 _____

12 _____

13 _____

VO Compounds

A Circle the verbs that are VO compounds.

吃飯   跳舞   工作   認識   請客

Communication

A Interview your classmates, jot down the information you gather, then present an oral or written report to introduce them to the class. Below are sample questions to help you get started.

Personal and Family Background

1 你今年多大？

_____

2 你的生日（是）幾月幾號？

_____

3 你是紐約人嗎？ _____

4 你家有幾口人？有沒有兄 *(xiōng)* (older brother) 弟姐妹？

_____

5 你爸爸、媽媽做什麼工作？他們在哪兒工作？

_____

Likes and Dislikes

1 你喜歡做什麼？打球還是看電影？

_____

2 你覺得做什麼有意思／沒有意思？

_____

3 你喜歡聽音樂嗎？ _____

4 你喜歡聽誰的音樂？ _____

5 你喜歡跳舞嗎？ _____

6 你喜歡跳什麼舞？ _____

7 你喜歡喝什麼？水、茶、可樂還是咖啡？

_____

Habits and Routines

1 你常常看電視嗎？ _____

2 你常常在哪兒看書？ _____

3 你晚上常常幾點睡覺？ _____

4 你週末常常做什麼？ _____

Lesson 6

第六課

約時間
Making Appointments

Check off the following items as you learn them.

Useful Expressions

[ ] What's going on?

[ ] Are you free tomorrow?

[ ] I'll wait for your call.

[ ] No problem.

[ ] You're welcome.

Cultural Norms

[ ] Honorifics

[ ] Phone etiquette

[ ] Popular messaging apps

[ ] China Standard Time (CST)

As you progress through the lesson, note other useful expressions and cultural norms you would like to learn.

_____

_____

_____

Dialogue 1: Calling Your Teacher

Audio

Listening Comprehension

A Listen to the Textbook Dialogue 1 audio, then circle the most appropriate choice. INTERPRETIVE

1 Why is Li You calling Teacher Chang?

   a Li You cannot come to school because she is sick.

   b Li You wants to ask some questions.

   c Li You wants to know where Teacher Chang's office is.

   d Li You wants to know where the meeting is.

2 What is Teacher Chang going to do this afternoon?

   a teach two classes

   b go home early

   c attend a meeting

   d go to a doctor's appointment

3 How many classes will Teacher Chang teach tomorrow morning?

   a one

   b two

   c three

   d four

4 What will Teacher Chang be doing at 3:30 tomorrow afternoon?

   a attending a meeting

   b giving an exam

   c working in her office

   d seeing a doctor

5 Where is Li You going to meet Teacher Chang?

   a in Teacher Chang's office

   b in the classroom

   c in the meeting room

   d in the library

6 When will Li You meet with Teacher Chang tomorrow?

   a 9:00 a.m.

   b 10:30 a.m.

   c 3:00 p.m.

   d 4:30 p.m.

B Listen to the Workbook Dialogue 1 audio, then mark these statements true or false. INTERPRETIVE

1 _____ The woman in the dialogue is the caller's sister.

2 _____ The caller asks to speak to Little Gao.

3 _____ A Chinese film will be screened tonight.

4 _____ The woman will most likely stay home tonight.

C Listen to the Workbook Dialogue 2 audio, then circle the most appropriate choice. INTERPRETIVE

1 Which of the following statements is true?

  a The woman invites the man to a dinner party at her home.

  b The woman invites the man to a dance at her home.

  c The woman hopes to go to a dinner party at the man's home.

  d The woman hopes to go to a dance at the man's home.

2 Why does the man choose not to go?

  a Because he is hosting a party.

  b Because he has to prepare for a test.

  c Because he is not allowed to go.

  d Because he doesn't like the host.

Pinyin and Tone

A Identify the characters with the same initials (either *j* or *sh*) and write them in *pinyin*.

試　間　上　時　節　級

1 *j:* _____

2 *sh:* _____

B Compare the tones of these characters. Indicate the tones with 1 (first tone), 2 (second tone), 3 (third tone), 4 (fourth tone), or 0 (neutral tone).

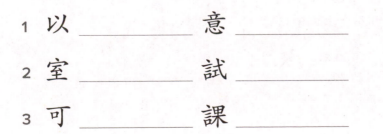

1 以 _____ 意 _____

2 室 _____ 試 _____

3 可 _____ 課 _____

A Answer these questions in Chinese based on Textbook Dialogue 1. PRESENTATIONAL

1 Why did Li You call Teacher Chang?

2 Will Teacher Chang be free this afternoon? Why or why not?

3 Will Teacher Chang be free tomorrow morning? Why or why not?

4 What will Teacher Chang do at three o'clock tomorrow afternoon?

5 When will Li You go to visit Teacher Chang?

B Have a conversation with your teacher. You would like to make an appointment, but he/she is busy at the time you suggest. Ask when he/she will be available. Decide on a time and place to meet. INTERPERSONAL

Reading Comprehension

A Match the sentences below with the responses that follow. INTERPRETIVE

1 _____ 你是哪位？

2 _____ 我們今天晚上去跳舞，好嗎？

3 _____ 喝點兒茶，怎麼樣？

4 _____ 喂，請問小白在嗎？

5 _____ 認識你很高興。

6 _____ 謝謝。

7 _____ 明天見。

8 _____ 今天下午我來找你，好嗎？

a 認識你們我也很高興。

b 不客氣。

c 再見。

d 對不起，我不喜歡喝茶。

e 對不起，她去圖書館了。

f 對不起，我今天下午要開會。

g 對不起，我明天要考試。

h 我是王朋。

B Read Teacher Li's schedule, then answer the questions in English. INTERPRETIVE

小高的中文老師李老師很忙。我們一起看一下她星期三做什麼。

8:30	到學校去上課	
9:00 - 10:00	上一年級中文課	
10:15 - 11:00	去圖書館找書	
12:00 - 1:00	在辦公室吃飯	
1:30 - 2:30	上二年級中文課	
2:45 - 3:30	開會	
4:00 - 5:00	學生來她的辦公室問問題	

1 李老師星期三有幾節課？

_____

2 李老師的學生星期三有沒有考試？

_____

3 李老師回家吃午飯 (wǔfàn) (lunch) 嗎？

_____

4 李老師上了一年級中文課以後做什麼？

_____

5 要是小高想去李老師的辦公室問問題，
  什麼時候去方便？

_____

6 你覺得李老師星期三幾點才可以回家？

_____

C Read this dialogue, then mark the statements true or false. INTERPRETIVE

（李友給王朋打電話。李友問了王朋幾個
問題。）

王朋：還有別的問題嗎？

李友：我還有一個問題。

王朋：你問吧。

李友：你明天下午有空嗎？我想找你聊
　　　天兒。

王朋：對不起，我明天下午要開會。

李友：明天晚上怎麼樣？

王朋：我明天晚上也沒有時間。我想請一個女孩子去跳舞。

李友：……那算了。

王朋：你也認識那個女孩子。

李友：是嗎？她叫什麼名字？

王朋：她姓李，叫李友。

1 ____ Li You's schedule for tomorrow seems quite flexible.

2 ____ Wang Peng hopes to see Li You tomorrow.

3 ____ Li You does not know the girl whom Wang Peng wants to take to the dance.

D Based on the dialogue in (C), circle the most appropriate choice.

1 What will Wang Peng do tomorrow?

a He will have a meeting in the afternoon and chat with Li You in the evening.

b He will meet with Li You in the afternoon and go dancing with another girl in the evening.

c He will have a meeting in the afternoon and go dancing with Li You in the evening.

2 On hearing Wang Peng's plan for tomorrow evening, how is Li You feeling?

a first disappointed and then very happy

b first very happy and then disappointed

c neither happy nor disappointed

Writing and Grammar

A Which of these characters in the group below are based on the top-bottom pattern, and which on the semi-enclosing pattern? After identifying the patterns, write the characters and their common radicals in the spaces provided (write the common radicals in 3 and 6).

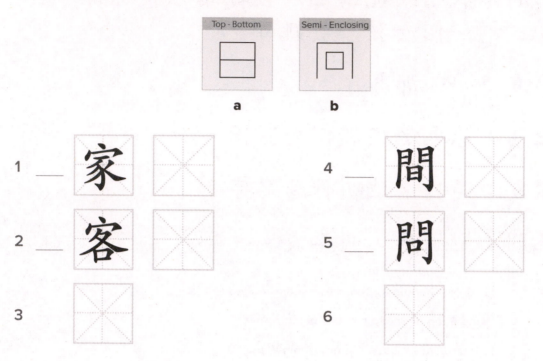

Top - Bottom	Semi - Enclosing
a	b

1 ___ 家

2 ___ 客

3

4 ___ 間

5 ___ 問

6

B Describe the images by writing the appropriate numbers, measure words, and nouns. Follow the example below. PRESENTATIONAL

兩個問題

1 _____

2 _____

3 _____

4 _____

C Use 要是 and the information below to form questions about how you would like to spend your free time. Follow the example below. PRESENTATIONAL

沒課

Q: 要是你明天沒課，你做什麼？

A: 我（去）（圖書館）看書。

1 沒事兒

Q: _____ ?

A: _____ 。

2 有空兒

Q: _____ ?

A: _____ 。

3 不開會

Q: _____ ?

A: _____ 。

4 不考試

Q: _____ ?

A: _____ 。

5 不工作

Q: _____ ?

A: _____ 。

D Translate these sentences into Chinese. PRESENTATIONAL

1 **Student A:** I'd like to give him a call.

_____

Student B: Don't call. He is not home right now.

_____

Student A: Really? When will he be home?

_____

Student B: He won't go home until after 5:00 p.m.

_____

2 Student A: Miss Bai, do you have time tomorrow?

_____

Student B: I am free tomorrow. What's the matter?

_____

Student A: I'd like to treat you to a movie.

_____

Student B: Watching movies is boring. Let's go dancing.

_____

Student A: No problem. See you tomorrow.

_____

3 Gao Wenzhong: Hello! Is Teacher Chang there?

_____

Teacher Chang: This is she. Who's this, please?

_____

Gao Wenzhong: Teacher Chang, how are you? This is Gao Wenzhong.

_____

Teacher Chang: Hi, Gao Wenzhong, what is it?

_____

Gao Wenzhong: I'd like to go to your office right now to ask you a question. Is that okay?

_____

Teacher Chang: Sure. I'll wait for you in my office.

_____

Gao Wenzhong: Thanks.

_____

 E   Ask your teacher what his/her typical school day is like. Take notes and transcribe what he/she said.
PRESENTATIONAL

_____

_____

_____

Dialogue 2: Calling a Friend for Help

Listening Comprehension

A   Listen to the Textbook Dialogue 2 audio, then mark these statements true or false. INTERPRETIVE

1 _____ Li You is returning Wang Peng's phone call.

2 _____ Li You has an exam next week.

3 _____ Li You asks Wang Peng to practice Chinese with her.

4 _____ Wang Peng invites Li You to have coffee.

5 _____ Wang Peng is going to have dinner with Li You this evening.

6 _____ Wang Peng does not know exactly when he is going to call Li You.

B   Listen to the Workbook Dialogue 1 audio, then mark these statements true or false. INTERPRETIVE

1 _____ Tomorrow is Friday.

2 _____ Li You cannot go to the dinner tomorrow because she will be busy.

3 _____ Li You will be practicing Chinese this evening.

4 _____ Wang Peng promises to help Li You with her Chinese tomorrow at 6:30 p.m.

C   Listen to the Workbook Dialogue 2 audio, then mark these statements true or false. INTERPRETIVE

1 _____ Wang Peng cannot help Li You because he has class tomorrow afternoon.

2 _____ Wang Peng asks Little Bai to help Li You with her Chinese.

3 _____ Little Bai and Li You will meet at 2 p.m. tomorrow in the library.

Pinyin and Tone

A   Identify the characters with the same finals (either *ie* or *ian*) and write them in *pinyin*.

節　間　便　別　練　面

1 *ie:* _____

2 *ian:* _____

Compare the tones of these characters. Indicate the tones with 1 (first tone), 2 (second tone), 3 (third tone), 4 (fourth tone), or 0 (neutral tone).

1 會 _____ 回 _____   3 習 _____ 喜 _____

2 問 _____ 文 _____   4 行 _____ 姓 _____

Speaking

A Answer these questions in Chinese based on Textbook Dialogue 2. PRESENTATIONAL

1 Why did Li You call Wang Peng?

2 Why did Wang Peng ask Li You to invite him for coffee?

3 What will Wang Peng do tonight?

4 Will Wang Peng meet with Li You tonight?

5 What will Li You do tonight?

B In pairs, role-play a phone call. Call your partner for a favor and promise something in return. You would like to meet him/her tonight, but he/she is going to see a movie. He/she promises to give you a call later. INTERPERSONAL

Reading Comprehension

A Review Little Gao's plans for next week, then answer the questions in English. INTERPRETIVE

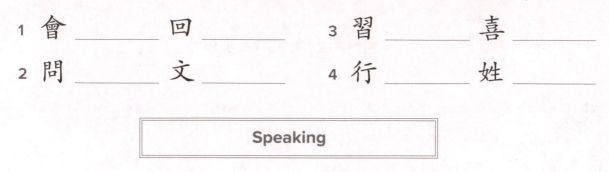

1 他什麼時候考中文？

_____

2 他跟王朋在哪兒練習中文？

_____

3 他為什麼星期五要打電話回家？

_____

4 他星期幾沒事兒？

_____

5 他星期四要做什麼？

_____

6 他星期天在哪兒吃飯？

_____

B Read this email, then mark the statements true or false. INTERPRETIVE

小白：

　　我下午在圖書館等你，可是你沒來。我四點給你打了一個電話，可是你不在家。我們什麼時候可以見面？我明天晚上要跟小王一起去看電影。要是你明天晚上有空，我可以不去看電影。今天晚上在家等你的電話。

小高

1 _____ Little Bai and Little Gao were in the library this afternoon.

2 _____ Little Bai did not leave her dorm until 4:00 p.m.

3 _____ Little Gao wants to see Little Bai.

4 _____ We do not know for sure what Little Gao will be doing tomorrow evening.

5 ____ Little Gao considers an appointment with Little Bai more important than seeing a movie with Little Wang.

6 ____ Little Gao will call Little Bai again this evening.

C Read this note that Little Bai left for Wang Peng, then answer the questions in English. INTERPRETIVE

王朋：

　　你今天下午沒有課，我來找你，可是你不在。我昨天到常老師的辦公室去，請她幫我練習說中文，可是她很忙。我今天上午給老師打電話，問她今天下午方便不方便，她說她明天下午兩點以後才有空兒。我明天上午要考中文，你可以幫我準備一下嗎？請你回來以後給我打電話。謝謝!

小白

五點半

1 Where did Wang Peng find this note?

_____

2 When was this note written?

_____

3 Why didn't Little Bai call before dropping by?

_____

4 Why did Little Bai go looking for Wang Peng?

_____

5 Did Little Bai get help from her teacher? Explain the situation.

_____

6 What do you think Wang Peng will do after he reads this note?

_____

D After reading the note in (C), Wang Peng found another one. Read it, then mark the statements true or false. INTERPRETIVE

王朋：

　　李友今天下午兩點半給你打電話說她今天下午兩點才知道星期五上午有中文考試，所以今天晚上不跟你去跳舞。要是你有空，她想請你今天下午幫她練習中文，她考試以後請你看電影。你回來以後給她打電話吧。

小高

兩點三刻

1 ____ This note was left by Li You.

2 ____ Wang Peng was not in at 2:30 p.m. but was back by 2:45 p.m.

3 ____ At 1:30 p.m. today Li You still planned to go to the dance.

4 ____ We do not know when Wang Peng will call Li You back.

5 ____ Li You was certain that Wang Peng would be available this afternoon.

E Based on the note in (D), circle the most appropriate choice. INTERPRETIVE

1 **Which of the statements is true?**
   a   Li You was told last Friday that there would be an exam.
   b   Li You was told this afternoon that there would be an exam on Friday.
   c   Li You was told that yesterday evening's exam was postponed till Friday.

2 **When does Li You hope to take Wang Peng to a movie?**
   a   Wednesday evening
   b   Thursday evening
   c   Friday evening

A Write the common radical and the characters, then provide the characters' meanings. Consider their relationship with the radical.

話　請　說

1 ⬚

2 ⬚ _____

3 ⬚ _____

4 ⬚ _____

B Make sentences using 別, 得, and the given words. Follow the example below. PRESENTATIONAL

Student A: 我想去找同學聊天兒。（準備考試）

Student B: <u>別</u>去找同學聊天，你<u>得</u>準備考試。

1 Student A: 我想看電視。（看書）

Student B: _____

2 Student A: 我想喝咖啡。（睡覺）

Student B: _____

3 Student A: 我想跟朋友玩兒。（工作）

Student B: _____

C Answer these questions according to your own circumstances. INTERPERSONAL

1 你常常給誰打電話？

_____

2 你是大學幾年級的學生？

_____

3 你星期一有幾節課？

_____

4 你星期四幾點有中文課？

_____

5 你常常跟誰一起練習說中文？

_____

D Rearrange these Chinese words into sentences, using the English sentences as clues.

PRESENTATIONAL

1 四點 | 我 | 辦公室 | 電話 | 在 | 明天 | 等 | 以後 | 下午 | 你的

(I will be waiting for your phone call in the office after 4:00 p.m. tomorrow.)

_____

2 朋友 | 才 | 吃飯 | 昨天晚上 | 我 | 回來 | 晚上九點 | 請我

(My friend took me out for dinner last night. I didn't come back until 9:00 p.m.)

_____

3 您 | 回來 | 給我 | 方便 | 以後 | 打 | 要是 | 電話

(If it is convenient for you, please give me a call after you come back.)

_____

E Translate these sentences into Chinese. **PRESENTATIONAL**

1 **Student A:**　Do you know Miss Chang?

_____

Student B:　I don't know her.

_____

Student A:　This is a photo of Miss Chang.

_____

Student B:　She is tall and pretty. I'd like to meet her.

Student A: No problem. I'll call her now.

_____

Student B: Great!

_____

2 Student A: I have a meeting tomorrow. Help me prepare, okay?

_____

Student B: Sure, I will help you after dinner. Could you wait a bit?

_____

Student A: Okay, I'll wait for you.

_____

3 Student A: When are you free today?

_____

Student B: I have three classes today, and won't be free until after 2:30 p.m. What's the matter?

_____

Student A: I'd like to ask you to practice Chinese with me.

_____

Student B: Okay, I'll wait for you at the library at 3:00 p.m.

_____

F   Write an email to your classmate to see if he/she can practice Chinese with you tomorrow evening. Promise your classmate that you will buy him/her a cup of coffee afterwards. PRESENTATIONAL

_____

_____

_____

G   Plan a perfect date. Indicate where and when you wish to meet with your date, and list what you would like to do by using the sentence pattern "A 跟 B + V(O)." PRESENTATIONAL

_____

_____

_____

Lesson 7

第七課

學中文
Studying Chinese

 Check off the following items as you learn them.

Useful Expressions

[ ] Good morning.

[ ] How about it?

[ ] That would be great!

[ ] I'm flattered.

[ ] That's so cool.

Cultural Norms

[ ] Accepting compliments

[ ] Character-writing systems

[ ] Traditional writing instruments

[ ] Value placed on education

As you progress through the lesson, note other useful expressions and cultural norms you would like to learn.

_____

_____

_____

Dialogue 1:
How Did You Do on the Exam?

Audio

Listening Comprehension

A Listen to the Textbook Dialogue 1 audio, then mark these statements true or false. INTERPRETIVE

1 _____ Li You didn't do well on her test last week.

2 _____ Wang Peng writes Chinese characters well, but very slowly.

3 _____ Wang Peng didn't want to teach Li You how to write Chinese characters.

4 _____ Li You has gone over tomorrow's lesson.

5 _____ The Chinese characters in Lesson 7 are very easy.

6 _____ Li You has no problems with Lesson 7's grammar.

B Listen to the Workbook Narrative audio, then mark these statements true or false. INTERPRETIVE

1 _____ Mr. Li likes studying Chinese, but not English.

2 _____ Mr. Li feels that English grammar is not too difficult, but Chinese grammar is hard.

3 _____ Mr. Li has some difficulty with Chinese characters.

C Listen to the Workbook Dialogue audio, then mark these statements true or false. INTERPRETIVE

1 _____ The woman didn't do very well on the Chinese test last week.

2 _____ The woman confessed that she spent a lot of time watching TV.

3 _____ The man thinks that the woman should have been more prepared.

4 _____ The woman thinks that the man was too busy to help her.

Pinyin and Tone

A Identify the characters with the same initials (either *zh* or *x*) and write them in *pinyin*.

學 習 枝 紙 寫 張 真

1 *zh:* _____

2 *x:* _____

B Compare the tones of these characters. Indicate the tones with 1 (first tone), 2 (second tone), 3 (third tone), 4 (fourth tone), or 0 (neutral tone).

1 紙 _____ 只 _____

2 字 _____ 子 _____

3 難 _____ 男 _____

Speaking

A Answer these questions in Chinese based on Textbook Dialogue 1. PRESENTATIONAL

1 How did Li You do on last week's test? Why?

2 Why does Wang Peng offer to help Li You with her writing of Chinese characters?

3 Who writes Chinese characters quickly?

4 Which lesson will Li You study tomorrow?

5 How does Li You feel about the grammar, vocabulary, and characters in the lesson she has prepared?

6 What will Wang Peng and Li You do tonight?

B Comment on the grammar, vocabulary, and characters in the last lesson you studied. PRESENTATIONAL

C In pairs, discuss the result of your recent Chinese test. Comment on how you did in learning the grammar, reviewing the vocabulary, and writing the characters. INTERPERSONAL

A Read this note that Little Bai left for Little Wang, then mark the statements true or false. INTERPRETIVE

小王：

你好！我上個星期有個中文考試，我考得不太好。我寫漢字寫得不錯，可是太慢。中文語法也有一點兒難，我不太懂。這個週末你有時間嗎？我想請你幫我復習中文。好嗎？

小白

1 ____ Little Bai did well on the exam.

2 ____ Little Bai wrote the characters pretty well, although slowly.

3 ____ Little Bai didn't understand the grammar at all.

4 ____ Little Bai hoped to see Little Wang this afternoon.

5 ____ Little Wang's Chinese seems to be better than Little Bai's.

B Read this passage written by a student, then mark the statements true or false. INTERPRETIVE

我們都不喜歡考試，但是我們的中文老師常常給我們考試。我們喜歡唱歌、跳舞，可是我們的老師不唱歌，也不跳舞，很沒有意思。她說我們得常常聽中文、練習說中文。要是我們聽了、練習了，她就很高興。要是我們沒聽、沒練習，她就很不高興。有的時候，我們還得去她的辦公室請她幫我們復習。要是老師不來學校上課，不給我們考試，在家喝茶、看電視、聊天，那不是很好嗎？

1 ____ The narrator considers her attitude toward tests representative of her fellow students.

2 ____ The teacher is popular because she and the students have similar hobbies.

3 ____ The teacher seems to care a lot about her students' education.

4 ____ The students often have tea with the teacher in her office.

5 ____ The teacher has decided not to give tests to the students anymore.

6 ____ The narrator hopes the teacher will invite the students to visit her home.

C Read this passage, then mark the statements true or false. INTERPRETIVE

昨天是小高的生日，李友和王朋都到小高家去了。他們一起喝茶、聽音樂、唱歌，晚上十二點才回家。王朋因為喝了很多茶，所以睡覺睡得不好。李友因為昨天沒有準備，所以今天考試考得不好。

1 ____ Both Wang Peng and Li You went to Little Gao's place.

2 ____ Wang Peng, Li You, and Little Gao were out yesterday evening.

3 ____ Wang Peng was the only one who drank tea last night.

4 ____ Wang Peng didn't sleep well last night because he had too much cola.

5 ____ Li You didn't have time yesterday to prepare for today's test.

D Would you be interested in reading this book? Why or why not? INTERPRETIVE

A Write the *pinyin* for the characters in the top row, compare them with the *pinyin* of the characters below, then consider the relationship between each pair.

1 字 _____ 2 慢 _____ 3 枝 _____

  子 *(zǐ)*   曼 *(màn)*   支 *(zhī)*

4 懂 _____ 5 張 _____ 6 試 _____

  董 *(dǒng)*   長 *(zhǎng)*   式 *(shì)*

B Draw a line connecting the object with its proper measure word. PRESENTATIONAL

1    一位

2    一杯

3    一瓶

4   一枝

5   一張

C What kinds of praise have you received or would you like to receive from your teacher, friends, or classmates? List them by using 得, following the example below. PRESENTATIONAL

說中文|好

你說中文說得很好。

1 打球|很好 _____

2 寫字|漂亮 _____

3 說英文|快 _____

4 考試|好 _____

5 預習生詞語法|不錯 _____

D Based on the images, write sentences about giving. Follow the example below. PRESENTATIONAL

 給王朋一瓶可樂。

1  _____

2 _____

3  _____

4 _____

Fill in the blanks with the numbered words. Each word may be used only once. PRESENTATIONAL

1 太   5 一起

2 有一點兒   6 常常

3 都   7 可是

4 也

我和我的姐姐＿＿＿＿＿喜歡聽音樂。我
們＿＿＿＿＿ ＿＿＿＿＿聽。我們＿＿＿＿＿喜
歡學中文。＿＿＿＿＿中國人說中文說
得＿＿＿＿＿快。我覺得語法也＿＿＿＿＿難。

F Which of these tasks are urgent enough that you think you should do them right away?
Select four to make sentences, following the example below. PRESENTATIONAL

a 去同學家玩兒   f 練習說中文

b 跟男／女朋友見面   g 練習寫漢字

c 跟媽媽說話   h 準備考試

d 回家睡覺   i 預習生詞語法

e 去學校開會

Task: 給爸爸打電話

我<u>現在就</u>給爸爸打電話。

1 ＿＿＿＿＿＿＿＿＿＿＿＿＿＿＿＿＿＿＿＿＿＿＿＿＿

2 ＿＿＿＿＿＿＿＿＿＿＿＿＿＿＿＿＿＿＿＿＿＿＿＿＿

3 ＿＿＿＿＿＿＿＿＿＿＿＿＿＿＿＿＿＿＿＿＿＿＿＿＿

4 ＿＿＿＿＿＿＿＿＿＿＿＿＿＿＿＿＿＿＿＿＿＿＿＿＿

G Translate these sentences into Chinese. PRESENTATIONAL

1 **Student A:** I think Chinese is interesting.

_____

Student B: But I feel that Chinese grammar is a bit hard.

_____

2 **Student A:** How about you teach me how to write characters?

_____

Student B: OK, give me a pen. Let's write them now.

_____

3 **Student A:** How did you do on the test?

_____

Student B: I reviewed Lesson 6 well, so I did well.

_____

4 **Student A:** I write Chinese characters way too slowly.

_____

Student B: I speak Chinese way too slowly.

_____

5 **Student A:** Could you help me practice speaking Chinese?

_____

Student B: I speak Chinese poorly. Let's go to the teacher's office and ask the teacher to help us.

_____

Student A: OK. We'll go find him now.

_____

H Comment on how well or how badly your family, classmates, friends, or any celebrities perform these activities. Follow the example below. PRESENTATIONAL

我覺得林書豪 *(Lín Shūháo)* (Jeremy Lin) 打球打得不錯。

1 打球 _____

2 唱歌 _____

3 跳舞 _____

4 工作 _____

5 說英文 _____

6 學中文 _____

7 預習生詞語法 _____

8 準備考試 _____

Dialogue 2:
Preparing for Chinese Class

Audio

| **Listening Comprehension** |

A Listen to the Textbook Dialogue 2 audio, then mark these statements true or false. INTERPRETIVE

1 _____ Bai Ying'ai is always late.

2 _____ Bai Ying'ai didn't go to bed until early this morning.

3 _____ Li You went to bed very late because she was studying Chinese.

4 _____ Li You recited the lesson well because she listened to the audio the night before.

5 _____ According to Bai Ying'ai, Li You has a very handsome Chinese friend.

B Listen to the Workbook Dialogue audio, then mark these statements true or false. INTERPRETIVE

1 _____ The man usually comes early.

2 _____ The man previewed Lesson 8.

3 _____ The man went to bed early because he didn't have homework last night.

4 _____ The man usually goes to bed around 9:00 p.m.

| **Pinyin and Tone** |

A Identify the characters with the same finals (either *an* or *ang*) and write them in *pinyin*.

晚　上　慢　張　漢　難

1 *an:* _____

2 *ang:* _____

B Compare the tones of these characters. Indicate the tones with 1 (first tone), 2 (second tone), 3 (third tone), 4 (fourth tone), or 0 (neutral tone).

1 喜 _____ 習 _____　3 工 _____ 功 _____

2 紙 _____ 枝 _____　4 語 _____ 預 _____

Speaking

A Answer these questions in Chinese based on Textbook Dialogue 2. PRESENTATIONAL

1 Why did Bai Ying'ai come so late today?

2 Why was Li You able to go to bed early last night?

3 Why did Bai Ying'ai say that it is nice to have a Chinese friend?

4 Which lesson is the class studying today?

5 Who did not listen to the audio last night?

6 How did Bai Ying'ai describe Li You's friend?

B In pairs, have a conversation about scheduling. Find out if your partner was early or late for class, went to bed early or late, and prepared for today's lesson or not. INTERPERSONAL

Reading Comprehension

A Read Li You's schedule for today, then mark the statements true or false. INTERPRETIVE

上午	八點半	預習生詞
	九點一刻	聽錄音
	十點	上中文課
中午	十二點	吃午飯
下午	一點	睡覺
	兩點	復習中文
晚上	六點	吃晚飯
	八點	做功課

1 _____ 李友今天沒有課。

2 _____ 李友上午預習生詞。

3 _____ 李友下午聽錄音。

4 _____ 李友不吃午飯，只吃晚飯。

5 _____ 李友復習中文以後睡午覺。

6 _____ 李友吃晚飯以後做功課。

B Read this passage, then mark the statements true or false. INTERPRETIVE

今天上午，小李預習了第六課。第六課的語法有點兒難，生詞也很多。下午她要去老師的辦公室問問題。她覺得學中文很有意思，說中國話不太難，可是漢字有一點兒難。

1 ____ Little Li thinks Lesson 6 is hard.

2 ____ Little Li will go to her teacher's office today.

3 ____ Little Li's teacher will give her a test this afternoon.

4 ____ Little Li feels very frustrated with her Chinese.

5 ____ Little Li considers speaking Chinese easier than writing Chinese characters.

C Read this passage, then answer the questions by circling the most appropriate choice. INTERPRETIVE

小美是中國學生，在美國大學學英文。昨天下午她在圖書館做功課。她覺得英文生詞太多，語法也不容易。因為一個美國男學生幫她復習生詞和語法，所以她做功課做得很快。那個美國男生很帥，很酷。今天小美想給他打電話，才知道沒有問他的名字和電話。

1 Which of these statements about Xiaomei is true?

  a She is a Chinese student tutoring American students in Chinese.

  b She is an American student taking a Chinese class.

  c She is a Chinese student taking an English class.

  d She is an American student studying Chinese with Chinese students.

2 Which of these statements is true about her homework yesterday?

  a She completed it quickly because the grammar and vocabulary were easy.

  b She completed it quickly even though the grammar and vocabulary were difficult.

  c She completed it slowly because the grammar and vocabulary were difficult.

  d She completed it slowly even though the grammar and vocabulary were easy.

D Based on the passage from (C), mark these statements true or false. INTERPRETIVE

1 ____ We can assume that Xiaomei likes the young man she met.

2 ____ Xiaomei had the young man's phone number.

E How many of these books are about Chinese grammar and how many are about Chinese characters? INTERPRETIVE

> # Writing and Grammar

A Write the common radical and the characters, then compound each character with another one to form a disyllabic word that you have learned (write the common radicals in 1 and 5).

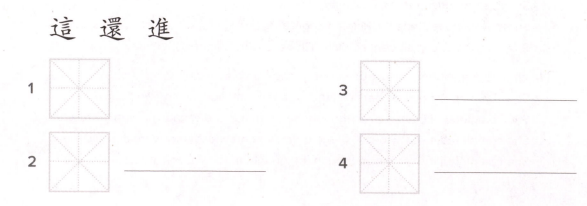

這　還　進

1 ▢ ____

2 ▢ ____

3 ▢ ____

4 ▢ ____

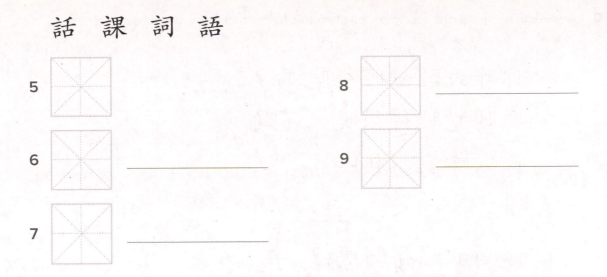

話 課 詞 語

5 □ _____   8 □ _____

6 □ _____   9 □ _____

7 □ _____

B When people give praise or make complaints, they often use 真 or 太. Fill in the blanks with the appropriate word. **PRESENTATIONAL**

1 老師說話說得____慢了，學生都不想聽。

2 功課____多，晚上得聽錄音、寫漢字。

3 早上七點半就得去學校上課，____早了。

4 你哥哥____帥，很多女孩子都想認識他。

5 小王寫漢字寫得____漂亮，我想請他教我怎麼寫。

6 你念課文念得____不錯，常常聽錄音吧？

7 李老師上課上得____好了，大家都喜歡上他的課。

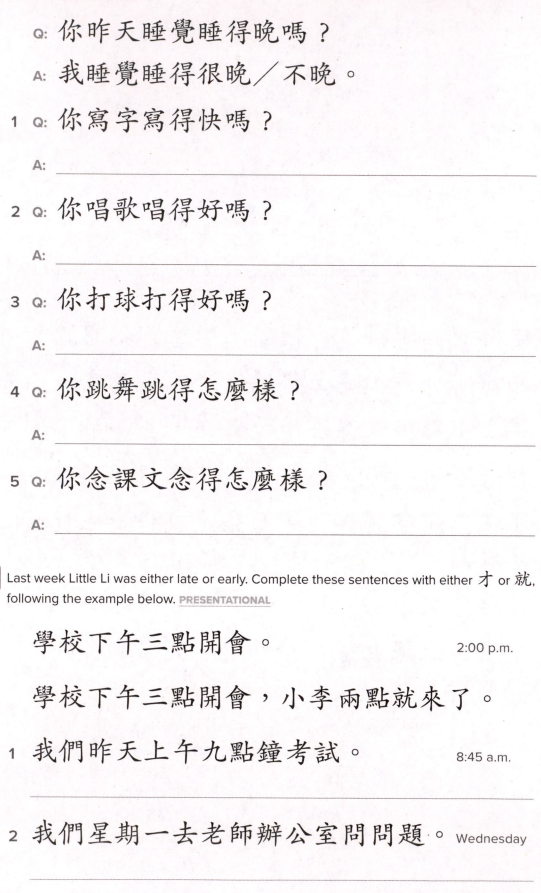

C Answer these questions according to your own circumstances, following the example below. INTERPERSONAL

Q: 你昨天睡覺睡得晚嗎？

A: 我睡覺睡得很晚／不晚。

1 Q: 你寫字寫得快嗎？

A: _____

2 Q: 你唱歌唱得好嗎？

A: _____

3 Q: 你打球打得好嗎？

A: _____

4 Q: 你跳舞跳得怎麼樣？

A: _____

5 Q: 你念課文念得怎麼樣？

A: _____

D Last week Little Li was either late or early. Complete these sentences with either 才 or 就, following the example below. PRESENTATIONAL

學校下午三點開會。   2:00 p.m.

學校下午三點開會，小李兩點就來了。

1 我們昨天上午九點鐘考試。   8:45 a.m.

_____

2 我們星期一去老師辦公室問問題。 Wednesday

_____

3 我們星期四預習生詞語法。   Tuesday

_____

4 我們昨天晚上十點回家。   11:30 p.m.

_____

E   Translate these sentences into Chinese. PRESENTATIONAL

 1   **Student A:**   How come you have so much homework tonight?

_____

     Student B: The teacher is going to give us a test tomorrow, and I have to review the text and practice writing Chinese.

_____

_____

 2   **Student A:**   Did you prepare Lesson 8 last night?

_____

     Student B: No, I didn't. I went to bed early at 9:30.

_____

     Student A: That was indeed early. I didn't go to bed until 1:30.

_____

     Student B: That's way too late.

_____

 3   **Student A:**   This is my boyfriend's picture.

_____

     Student B: He is very handsome.

_____

     Student A: He sings well, dances well, and plays ball well.

_____

     Student B: That's so cool!

F Is there a famous person you admire? List your idols and describe their appeal, following the example below. PRESENTATIONAL

林書豪 *(Lín Shūháo)* (Jeremy Lin) 真酷，他打球打得真好。

_____

_____

_____

_____

G Translate this passage into Chinese. PRESENTATIONAL

My younger sister did not learn Chinese well. She didn't like listening to the audio and didn't practice speaking, so she did not speak well. She didn't like studying grammar or writing characters. That was why she didn't do well on the exams. But after she met a Chinese friend, they often reviewed Chinese together in the library. Now, she likes listening to the audio and she also writes characters pretty well.

_____

_____

_____

_____

_____

學校生活
School Life

 Check off the following items as you learn them.

Useful Expressions

[ ] How are things recently?

[ ] What time are we going?

[ ] I hope you can come.

[ ] Please don't poke fun at me.

[ ] Wishing you all the best.

Cultural Norms

[ ] College entrance exams

[ ] School schedules

[ ] Formal writing conventions

As you progress through the lesson, note other useful expressions and cultural norms you would like to learn.

_____

_____

_____

Diary Entry: A Typical School Day

Audio

Listening Comprehension

A Listen to the Textbook Diary Entry audio, then circle the most appropriate choice. INTERPRETIVE

1 What did Li You do this morning before breakfast?

   a She took a bath.

   b She listened to the audio.

   c She checked her email.

   d She talked to her friend on the phone.

2 What time did Li You go to class this morning?

   a 7:30

   b 8:00

   c 8:30

   d 9:00

3 What did Li You not do in her Chinese class?

   a take a test

   b practice pronunciation

   c learn vocabulary

   d study grammar

4 Where did Li You have lunch today?

   a at a Chinese restaurant

   b at the school cafeteria

   c at home

   d at her friend's house

5 What was Li You doing around 4:30 p.m.?

   a practicing Chinese

   b checking her email

   c playing ball

   d drinking coffee

6 What time did Li You eat dinner?

   a 5:45

   b 6:00

   c 6:30

   d 7:30

7 Why did Li You visit Bai Ying'ai's dorm?

   a to eat dinner

   b to play video games

   c to chat

   d to study

8 What time did Li You return to her place?

   a 7:30

   b 8:30

   c 9:30

   d 10:30

9 What did Li You do before she went to bed?

   a visit Little Bai

   b finish her homework

   c talk to Gao Wenzhong on the phone

   d study for her test

B Listen to the Textbook Diary Entry audio, then number the images in the correct sequence.
INTERPRETIVE

1 _____   2 _____   3 _____

C Listen to the Workbook Dialogue audio, then mark these statements true or false. INTERPRETIVE

1 _____ Li You is going to Teacher Zhang's office at 4:00 p.m. today.

2 _____ Wang Peng will be attending a class at 2:30 p.m. today.

3 _____ Li You plans to do research at the library this evening.

4 _____ Li You and Wang Peng will see each other in the library this evening.

> ## Pinyin and Tone

A Identify the characters with the same initials (either *j* or *q*) and write them in *pinyin*.

記　起　前　經　教　請

1 *j:* _____

2 *q:* _____

B Compare the tones of these characters. Indicate the tones with 1 (first tone), 2 (second tone), 3 (third tone), 4 (fourth tone), or 0 (neutral tone).

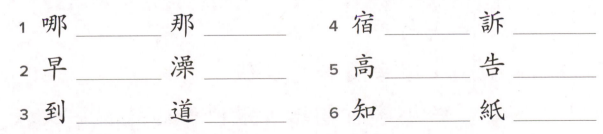

1 哪 _____ 那 _____   4 宿 _____ 訴 _____

2 早 _____ 澡 _____   5 高 _____ 告 _____

3 到 _____ 道 _____   6 知 _____ 紙 _____

Speaking

A Answer these questions in Chinese based on the Textbook Diary Entry. PRESENTATIONAL

1 What did Li You do after getting up?

2 Did Li You have breakfast?

3 How many classes did Li You have?

4 What did the teacher do in Li You's first class?

5 What did Li You do during her lunch hour?

6 What did Li You do at the library?

7 What did Li You do after dinner?

B In pairs, review this schedule and take turns describing what Wang Peng did yesterday morning.
INTERPERSONAL

Reading Comprehension

A Read this schedule for Little Wang, then mark the statements true or false. INTERPRETIVE

8:00 a.m.	復習第七課生詞、語法
9:00 a.m.	上電腦課
10:00 a.m.	去常老師的辦公室練習發音
2:30 p.m.	去圖書館看書
4:00 p.m.	去打球
6:00 p.m.	去宿舍餐廳吃晚飯
8:15 p.m.	給小李打電話，跟他一起練習中文
10:30 p.m.	給爸爸媽媽打電話
12:00 a.m.	睡覺

1 _____ 小王今天只有一節課。

2 _____ 小王跟小白一起吃午飯。

3 _____ 小王上午去找常老師。

4 _____ 小王去小李家練習中文。

5 _____ 小王吃晚飯以前去打球。

6 _____ 小王去圖書館以後去找常老師。

7 _____ 小王睡覺以前給爸爸媽媽打電話。

8 _____ 小王跟小李練習中文以後才吃飯。

B Read this passage, then mark the statements true or false. INTERPRETIVE

　　小高以前常常跟朋友一起打球、聊天、看電視，不做功課。可是因為他下星期要考試，所以這個星期他不打球、不看電視、也不找朋友聊天，一個人到圖書館去看書。他很早就起床，很晚才睡覺，所以他上課的時候常常想睡覺。

1 _____ 小高以前常常跟朋友一邊做功課，一邊聊天。

2 _____ 小高常常跟朋友一起到圖書館去看書。

3 _____ 因為小高要準備考試，所以他這個星期只看書，不玩兒。

4 _____ 小高覺得上課沒有意思，所以他上課的時候常常想睡覺。

5 _____ 這個星期小高睡覺睡得很早。

Read this dialogue, then mark the statements true or false. **INTERPRETIVE**

小李：你認識小常的男朋友文書明嗎？

小白：我認識。昨天我去圖書館上網的時候，他正在跟小常一起做功課。

小李：我也認識他，因為他跟我一起上電腦課。

小白：我覺得他很酷！

小李：他很帥，可是我不太喜歡他。

小白：是嗎？為什麼？

小李：別人說他有的時候一邊給小常打電話，一邊上網跟別的女孩子聊天。

小白：是嗎？小常知道不知道？你得告訴她！

1 ____ Little Bai is Little Chang's friend, but Little Li is not.

2 ____ Little Bai is in the same computer class as Wen Shuming.

3 ____ Little Chang and Wen Shuming did their homework together yesterday.

4 ____ Little Bai saw Little Li in the library yesterday.

5 ____ Little Li thinks Wen Shuming is handsome, but does not like him.

6 ____ At the end of the dialogue, Little Bai wants Little Li to talk to Little Chang.

A These characters all share the same radical, 糸 . Compound each of them with another character to form a disyllabic word, then write the meaning of the word in English.

1 經 _____ _____ 3 練 _____ _____

2 約 _____ _____ 4 紹 _____ _____

B Wang Peng is multi-talented and a good friend. Based on the images, state what he can teach his friends. Follow the example below. PRESENTATIONAL

王朋教朋友寫漢字。

1 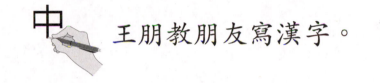 _____

2  _____

3  _____

4 _____

C Nowadays, people often multitask. Based on the images, describe what these people are doing. Follow the example below. PRESENTATIONAL

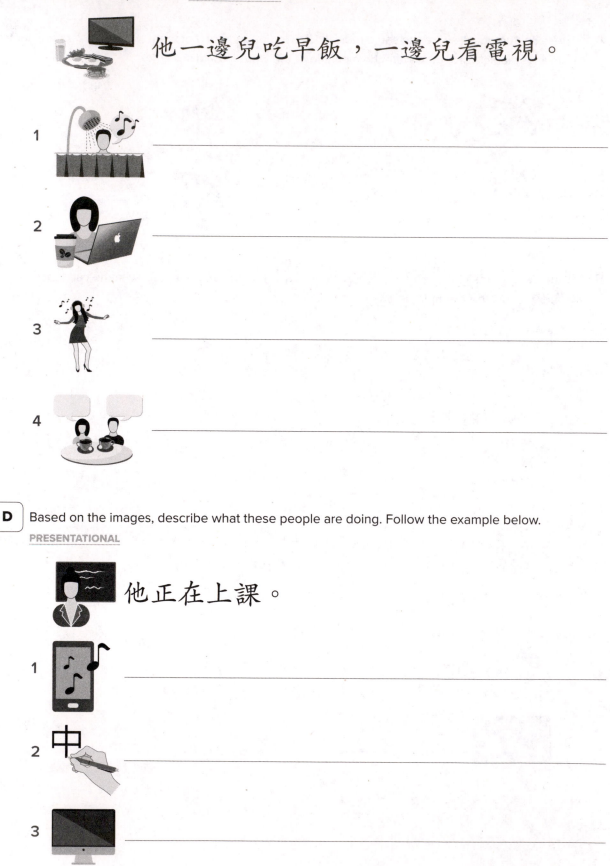

他一邊兒吃早飯，一邊兒看電視。

1 _____

2 _____

3 _____

4 _____

D Based on the images, describe what these people are doing. Follow the example below.
PRESENTATIONAL

他正在上課。

1 _____

2 _____

3 _____

4  _____

5 _____

E Translate these sentences into Chinese. PRESENTATIONAL

1 **Student A:** What do you want to do after class?

_____

   Student B: I want to go back to the dorm to do homework.

_____

2 **Student A:** You speak Chinese so well. Could you help me practice before tomorrow's test?

_____

   Student B: No problem. Let's have coffee and practice at the same time.

_____

3 **Student A:** This new text is a bit difficult.

_____

   Student B: Let's ask the teacher when we meet her tomorrow.

_____

4 **Student A:** I'll go to the cafeteria to have lunch right after the test. Have you had lunch already?

_____

   Student B: Don't wait for me. I have to work. I don't know when I'll have lunch today.

_____

F You are a newly hired personal assistant and your partner is your boss. Find out the following information so you can plan his/her schedule. INTERPERSONAL

1 When your boss gets up in the morning.

2 Whether your boss prefers to have breakfast at home or in the office.

3 When and with whom your boss has regular meetings.

4 What time your boss has lunch and dinner.

5 What time your boss plans to return home after work.

6 What time your boss goes to bed.

7 Any other daily activities that should be included in the schedule.

G After gathering your boss's information, you now need to enter it in your phone. PRESENTATIONAL

1 _____

2 _____

3 _____

4 _____

5 _____

6 _____

7 _____

H Describe your daily routine. PRESENTATIONAL

_____

_____

_____

_____

Letter: Writing to a Friend

Audio

Listening Comprehension

A Listen to the Textbook Letter audio, then mark these statements true or false. INTERPRETIVE

1 ____ This is a letter from Li You to Wang Peng.

2 ____ Li You's major is Chinese.

3 ____ Li You does not like her Chinese class at all.

4 ____ Li You's Chinese teacher speaks English very well.

5 ____ Li You is learning Chinese quickly because she has some help.

6 ____ Li You would like her friend to attend her school concert.

B Listen to the Workbook Narrative 1 audio, then mark these statements true or false. INTERPRETIVE

1 ____ Wang Peng went to the library to help Li You with her Chinese.

2 ____ Wang Peng did not go to play ball this afternoon until he had finished his homework.

3 ____ Li You went to a movie with Wang Peng this evening.

4 ____ Li You has a Chinese class tomorrow.

C Listen to the Workbook Narrative 2 audio that describes Little Li's activities yesterday, then place the letters representing those activities in the column to the right. INTERPRETIVE

a

b

c

d

1 _____

2 _____

3 _____

4 _____

e   5 _____

f   6 _____

g   7 _____

h   8 _____

Pinyin and Tone

A   Identify the characters with the same initials (either *j* or *zh*) and write them in *pinyin*.

祝　教　知　近　就　專　節

1   *j:* _____

2   *zh:* _____

B   Compare the tones of these characters. Indicate the tones with 1 (first tone), 2 (second tone), 3 (third tone), 4 (fourth tone), or 0 (neutral tone).

1 希 _____ 洗 _____   4 笑 _____ 小 _____

2 新 _____ 信 _____   5 網 _____ 望 _____

3 也 _____ 業 _____   6 醫 _____ 以 _____

Speaking

A Answer these questions in Chinese based on the Textbook Letter. PRESENTATIONAL

1 Why is Li You so busy this semester?

2 Describe Li You's Chinese class.

3 How did Li You feel about her Chinese class? Why?

4 Why did Li You ask Xiaoyin if she liked music?

B Describe your Chinese class to your friends in great detail. Make sure to comment on pronunciation, grammar, vocabulary, and Chinese characters. PRESENTATIONAL

Reading Comprehension

A Read this email, then answer the questions by circling the most appropriate choice. INTERPRETIVE

文書明：

　　你好！謝謝你那天在圖書館幫我復習英文語法。我的英文不好，請你別笑我。那天我不知道你的名字，但是後來我的朋友告訴我，你有一個漂亮的中文名字。我還知道，你這個字期除了電腦專業課以外，還在學中文。這個週末有一個中國電影，希望你能來看。有空的時候給我打個電話，好嗎？我的電話是555-5555。

小美

1 How does Xiaomei feel about her English?
   a   frustrated
   b   embarrassed
   c   proud

2 Where did Xiaomei get her information about Wen Shuming?

 a from Wen Shuming himself

 b from the librarian

 c from a friend

3 According to Xiaomei, which of the following facts about Wen Shuming is correct?

 a He is a computer science major who studies Chinese.

 b He is a Chinese major who studies computer science.

 c He is a student who majors in Chinese and computer science.

4 What does Xiaomei hope Wen Shuming will do?

 a come to see the movie but not call her

 b call her but not come to the movie

 c call her and come to the movie

B Read this passage, then mark the statements true or false. INTERPRETIVE

小高今天很忙，上午除了有三節課以外，還有一個電腦考試。他中午跟朋友一起吃飯，下午在圖書館看書、做功課，晚上在電腦室上網聊天兒，十點才回家吃晚飯。晚飯以後，他一邊看電視，一邊預習明天的功課，十二點半才睡覺。

1 _____ 小高上午沒空。

2 _____ 小高下午不在家，在圖書館工作。

3 _____ 小高晚上很晚才吃飯。

4 _____ 小高晚上在電腦室預習明天的功課。

5 _____ 小高一邊聽音樂，一邊看書。

Read this passage, then list five ways in which you are similar to or different from the narrator. Write your statements in English, starting with "Like the person" or "Unlike the person." INTERPRETIVE

我是大學一年級的學生。開始我不知道教室在哪兒，因為學校太大了；我不喜歡吃學校餐廳的飯，因為餐廳的飯太不好吃了；我也不會用學校圖書館的電腦，因為圖書館的電腦太新了；在宿舍洗澡也很不方便。中文課很難。除了生詞太多以外，我還覺得老師說話說得太快。

1 _____

2 _____

3 _____

4 _____

5 _____

Writing and Grammar

A You have just learned the character 用, which has the semi-enclosing pattern. Write three more characters in the same pattern, compound each of them with another character to form a disyllabic word, then translate the word into English.

Semi - Enclosing

1 ☐ _____ _____   3 ☐ _____ _____

2 ☐ _____ _____

Fill in the blanks with the appropriate measure words. Each measure word can only be used once.

PRESENTATIONAL

1 一 ＿＿＿＿ 老師　　　　6 一 ＿＿＿＿ 可樂

2 一 ＿＿＿＿ 照片　　　　7 一 ＿＿＿＿ 課

3 一 ＿＿＿＿ 電腦　　　　8 一 ＿＿＿＿ 課文

4 一 ＿＿＿＿ 筆　　　　　9 一 ＿＿＿＿ 信

5 一 ＿＿＿＿ 咖啡　　　　10 我家有三 ＿＿＿＿ 人。

C Answer these questions involving tools, methods, or means. Follow the example below.

INTERPERSONAL

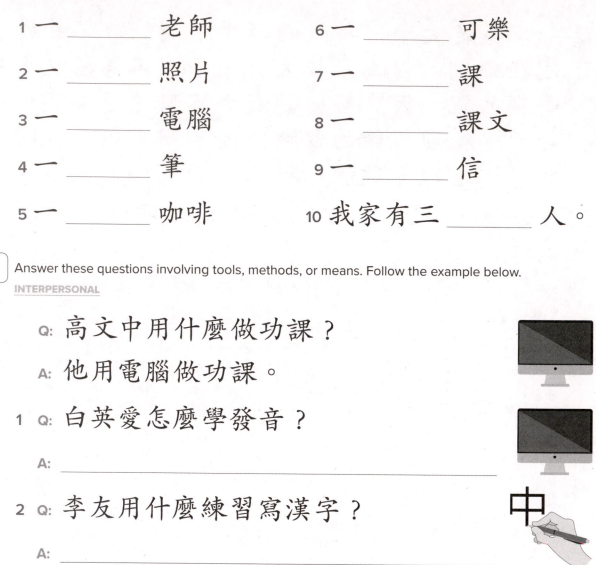

Q: 高文中用什麼做功課？

A: 他用電腦做功課。

1 Q: 白英愛怎麼學發音？

A: ＿＿＿＿＿＿＿＿＿＿＿＿＿＿＿＿＿＿＿＿＿＿＿＿＿

2 Q: 李友用什麼練習寫漢字？

A: ＿＿＿＿＿＿＿＿＿＿＿＿＿＿＿＿＿＿＿＿＿＿＿＿＿

3 Q: 高小音用中文還是英文寫信？

A: ＿＿＿＿＿＿＿＿＿＿＿＿＿＿＿＿＿＿＿＿＿＿＿＿＿

D Based on the images, list some of the things that Bai Ying'ai can do, and the one thing she cannot do. Follow the example below. PRESENTATIONAL

☑ 她會寫英文。

1 中 ☑ ＿＿＿＿＿＿＿＿＿＿＿＿＿＿＿＿＿＿＿＿＿＿＿＿＿

2 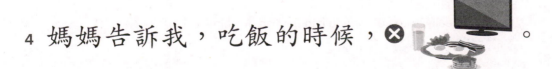 ✅ _____

3 ✅ _____

4 ❌ _____

<table>
<tr><td>E</td><td>Based on the images, list some activities that are typically forbidden at home or in class. Follow the example below. PRESENTATIONAL</td></tr>
</table>

老師告訴我，考試的時候，❌ 。

老師告訴我，考試的時候，<u>不能問問題</u>。

1 老師告訴我，上課的時候，❌ 。

_____

2 老師告訴我，上課的時候，❌ 。

_____

3 媽媽告訴我，做功課的時候，❌ 。

_____

4 媽媽告訴我，吃飯的時候，❌ 。

_____

F Describe what each person does or can do using "除了⋯以外，還⋯" Follow the example below. PRESENTATIONAL

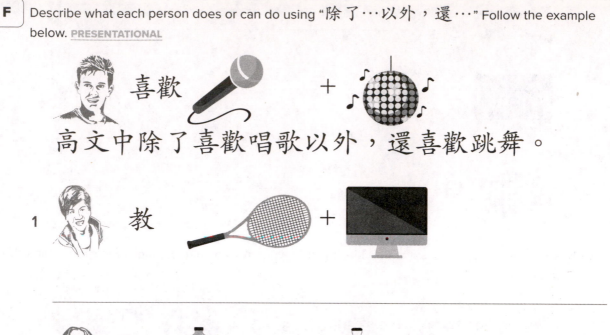

高文中除了喜歡唱歌以外，還喜歡跳舞。

1 教

_____

2 喝

_____

3 會 中

_____

G Translate these sentences into Chinese. PRESENTATIONAL

1 **Student A:** What are you doing?

_____

Student B: I am writing a letter to my friend.

_____

Student A: Really? Are you writing it in English or Chinese?

_____

Student B: I'm writing it in Chinese. She doesn't know English.

_____

2 Student A: Did Teacher Chang help you practice speaking Chinese yesterday?

_____

Student B: No. She was at a meeting when I got to her office.

_____

3 Student A: What's your major?

_____

Student B: My major is Chinese.

_____

Student A: Great! Can you teach me Chinese characters?

_____

Student B: OK, I'll help you right after my class.

_____

4 Student A: You write characters so quickly.

_____

Student B: At first, I wrote very slowly. But later, my oldest brother helped me practice. Now I write quickly.

_____

5 Student A: Tomorrow is the weekend. I hope you can go to a concert with me.

_____

Student B: I'm sorry. I can't go. I have to work.

_____

6 Student A: This grammar is a bit difficult. Do you understand it?

_____

Student B: Don't ask me, I don't understand it either.

_____

H Based on the images, write down what Little Wang did yesterday. PRESENTATIONAL

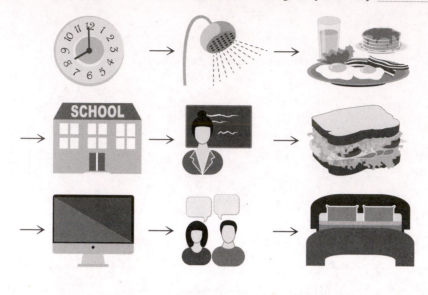

小王的一天

_____

_____

_____

_____

_____

I Write your friend an email in Chinese. Tell him/her about your experience learning Chinese. Include information about your study habits, in-class situation, after-class work, strengths and weaknesses, and likes and dislikes. Also comment on how your instructor teaches or how your classmates study. Don't forget to ask your friend about his/her studies, and wish him/her the best. PRESENTATIONAL

_____

_____

_____

_____

_____

買東西
Shopping

✓ Check off the following items as you learn them.

Useful Expressions

[ ] I'd like to buy a pair of shoes.

[ ] What color do you like?

[ ] What size?

[ ] I'll take them.

[ ] Can I use my credit card here?

Cultural Norms

[ ] Shopping etiquette

[ ] Popular e-commerce sites

[ ] Traditional clothing types

[ ] Denominations of currency

As you progress through the lesson, note other useful expressions and cultural norms you would like to learn.

_____

_____

_____

Dialogue 1: Shopping for Clothes

> ## Listening Comprehension

A Listen to the Textbook Dialogue 1 audio, then circle the most appropriate choice. INTERPRETIVE

1 What color shirt does Li You want to buy?

a black

b white

c red

d yellow

2 What else does Li You want to buy besides the shirt?

a a hat

b a pair of shoes

c a sweater

d a pair of pants

3 What size does Li You wear?

a small

b medium

c large

d extra large

4 How much does Li You need to pay altogether?

a between $20 and $30

b between $30 and $40

c between $40 and $50

d between $50 and $60

B Listen to the Workbook Narrative audio, then circle the most appropriate choice. INTERPRETIVE

1 What color does Wang Peng like?

a blue

b brown

c white

d red

2 Why doesn't Wang Peng like the shirt?

a It's too expensive.

b It's not stylish.

c He doesn't like the color.

d It doesn't fit.

3 What colors did the salesperson say they had?

    a white, blue, and brown

    b white, red, and brown

    c red, blue, and white

    d white, red, and yellow

4 When did Wang Peng buy the shirt?

    a five days ago

    b seven days ago

    c ten days ago

    d fourteen days ago

Pinyin and Tone

A Identify the characters with the same initials (either *ch* or *sh*) and write them in *pinyin*.

商　長　售　襯　衫　穿

1 *ch:* _____

2 *sh:* _____

B Compare the tones of these characters. Indicate the tones with 1 (first tone), 2 (second tone), 3 (third tone), 4 (fourth tone), or 0 (neutral tone).

1 衣 _____ 宜 _____　　**4** 商 _____ 上 _____

2 件 _____ 間 _____　　**5** 合 _____ 喝 _____

3 褲 _____ 酷 _____　　**6** 店 _____ 點 _____

Speaking

A Answer these questions in Chinese based on Textbook Dialogue 1. PRESENTATIONAL

1 What does Li You want to buy?

2 What color does Li You like?

3 What does Li You like about the pants?

4 Give the price for each item, and the total cost.

B In pairs, ask each other what size clothing you wear, what color you prefer, and the price of the clothing you are wearing. INTERPERSONAL

Reading Comprehension

A Read this passage, then mark the statements true or false. INTERPRETIVE

小文上個週末去買東西。他想買一件中號的紅襯衫，可是中號襯衫都是白的，紅襯衫都是大號的。售貨員很客氣，她幫小文找了一件襯衫，不是紅的，可是顏色不錯。那位售貨員告訴他，這件襯衫三十九塊九毛九。小文覺得有一點兒貴，可是他覺得要是不買就對不起那位售貨員，所以給了售貨員四十塊錢買了那件襯衫。

1 ＿＿ There were many items in the store for Little Wen to choose from.

2 ＿＿ The salesperson was very courteous.

3 ＿＿ Little Wen probably wears a size medium shirt.

4 ＿＿ Little Wen was looking for a white shirt.

5 ＿＿ The salesperson finally found a red shirt that Little Wen liked.

6 ＿＿ Little Wen bought the shirt because he didn't want to disappoint the salesperson.

B Read this dialogue, then mark the statements true or false. INTERPRETIVE

男：我今天買了一件襯衫，你看怎麼樣？

女：大小很合適，可是顏色不太好。你喜歡穿紅襯衫，怎麼買了這個顏色的？

男：我想買紅的，可是紅襯衫都太大了。

女：那你為什麼買這件？

男：因為那位售貨員……

女：很漂亮，對不對？

男：不，不，不。她不認識我，但是我知道她是你的朋友。

女：是嗎？

1 ____ The woman likes the color but not the size of the man's new shirt.

2 ____ The woman is somewhat surprised that the man bought that shirt.

3 ____ We can assume that many of the man's shirts are red.

4 ____ The man bought the shirt because the price was right.

5 ____ The salesperson turns out to be the man's friend.

C According to this index from a newspaper's classified section, on what page can you find ads for apparel? INTERPRETIVE

專項分類資訊 ▶▶▶			
二手房超市、租房手冊		音像軟件	79版
	36版	家居建材	81版
美好姻緣	54版	健康專遞	82版
招生廣場	66、69版	服裝服飾	82版
美容美髮招生	67版	五金、機械、化工	83版
擇業直通車	70、71版	印刷設計	83版
留學與移民	72版	快樂京郊遊	84版
汽車服務	75版	天天美容	84版

A Which of these characters are based on the top-bottom pattern, and which on the left-right pattern? After filling in the answers, write the characters in the spaces provided.

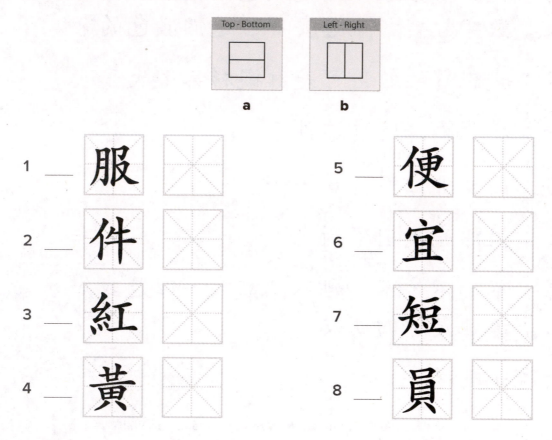

Top - Bottom	Left - Right
a	b

1 ___ 服

2 ___ 件

3 ___ 紅

4 ___ 黃

5 ___ 便

6 ___ 宜

7 ___ 短

8 ___ 員

B Based on the images, form question-and-answers about how much different items cost in your city. Follow the example below. **PRESENTATIONAL**

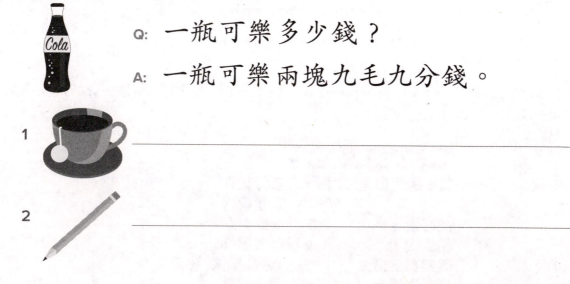

Q: 一瓶可樂多少錢？

A: 一瓶可樂兩塊九毛九分錢。

1 _____

2 _____

3 _____

4 _____

5 _____

C Based on the images, form question-and-answers about which items the IC characters prefer. Follow the example below. INTERPERSONAL

Q: 李友喜歡哪（一）件衣服？

A: 她喜歡白（色）的。

1 Q: 王朋要買哪（一）條褲子？

A: _____

2 Q: 高小音想喝哪杯茶？ ❌ $3.50 ✓ $2.00

A: _____

3 Q: 白英愛用哪枝筆？ ❌ ✓

A: _____

D Translate these sentences into Chinese. PRESENTATIONAL

1 Student A: This shirt is so pretty. Try it on.

_____

Student B: There's no need to. It's too expensive.

_____

2 Student A: What size pants do you wear?

_____

Student B: I wear size 30.

_____

3 Student A: Both the color and the length of the pants are right for you. Get them!

_____

Student B: I'll buy them if they are cheap.

_____

4 Student A: Miss, excuse me, how much is this medium-size shirt?

_____

Student B: It's twenty-nine dollars and fifty cents.

_____

Student A: Here's thirty dollars.

_____

Student B: Here's your change, fifty cents. Thank you.

_____

E Search the online catalog of a local clothing store. List the items you like. Include their colors, sizes, and prices. Bring a printout of the list and describe the items to the class. PRESENTATIONAL

_____

_____

_____

_____

F Describe the clothes you're wearing, including their colors and sizes. PRESENTATIONAL

_____

_____

_____

_____

Dialogue 2: Exchanging Shoes

Listening Comprehension

A Listen to the Textbook Dialogue 2 audio, then circle the most appropriate choice. INTERPRETIVE

1 Why does Wang Peng want to exchange the shoes?
   a The shoes do not fit well.
   b The shoes are damaged.
   c He does not like the price.
   d He does not like the color.

2 What color does Wang Peng prefer?
   a black
   b white
   c brown
   d red

3 In what way is the new pair of shoes like the old pair?
   a They are the same size.
   b They are the same color.
   c They are the same price.
   d They have the same design.

B Listen to the Workbook Dialogue 1 audio, then mark these statements true or false. INTERPRETIVE

1 _____ The man wants to return a shirt for a different one, because he doesn't like the color.

2 _____ The man finally takes a yellow shirt because he likes the color.

3 _____ All the large shirts in the store are yellow.

4 _____ A large shirt would fit the man well.

C Listen to the Workbook Dialogue 2 audio, then mark these statements true or false. INTERPRETIVE

1 _____ The store only sells clothes.

2 _____ The man knows what color and what size to get.

3 _____ The man seeks advice from the salesperson.

4 _____ The man wants to buy the most expensive shirt in the store.

5 _____ The man does not want to ruin the surprise for his girlfriend.

6 _____ The salesperson agrees with the man's choice.

Pinyin and Tone

A Identify the characters with the same finals (either *ou* or *uo*) and write them in *pinyin*.

都 多 說 售 貨 後 果

1 *ou:* _____

2 *uo:* _____

B Compare the tones of these characters. Indicate the tones with 1 (first tone), 2 (second tone), 3 (third tone), 4 (fourth tone), or 0 (neutral tone).

1 鞋 _____ 謝 _____   **4** 雖 _____ 歲 _____

2 種 _____ 中 _____   **5** 付 _____ 服 _____

3 過 _____ 果 _____

Speaking

A Answer these questions in Chinese based on Textbook Dialogue 2. PRESENTATIONAL

1 Why does Wang Peng want to return the shoes for a different pair?

2 Does Wang Peng like the black shoes? Why or why not?

3 What color shoes does Wang Peng finally take? Why?

4 Does Wang Peng pay any additional money for the new shoes? Why or why not?

B Describe the clothes you're wearing today, including their colors, sizes, and prices. PRESENTATIONAL

C In pairs, role-play a dialogue between a salesperson in a clothing store and a customer trying to exchange a shirt that's too large. Make sure that the size, color, and price are all correct. INTERPERSONAL

A Identify the items corresponding to the descriptions on the right. Place the correct letter next to its description.

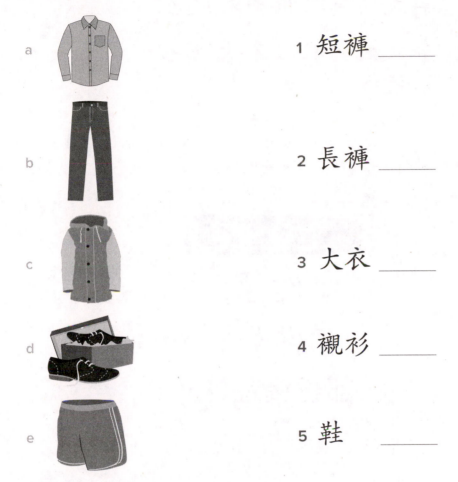

1 短褲 _____

2 長褲 _____

3 大衣 _____

4 襯衫 _____

5 鞋 _____

B Read this passage, then mark the statements true or false. INTERPRETIVE

　　李先生很喜歡買便宜的衣服。所以雖然他的衣服很多，可是他覺得都不太合適。李太太跟她先生不一樣。她不喜歡買東西，也不常買東西。李太太只買大小長短和顏色都合適的衣服，所以她的衣服雖然不多，可是她都喜歡。

1 _____ 李先生覺得買東西很有意思。

2 _____ 李先生的衣服很多，也都很貴。

3 _____ 李先生的衣服大小和顏色都很合適。

4 _____ 李太太覺得買衣服沒意思。

5 _____ 李太太買了很多衣服。

6 _____ 李太太的衣服不大也不小，不長也不短。

C Look at the sign, identify and circle the goods that are on sale, then explain (in either English or Chinese) what kinds of deals are being offered. INTERPRETIVE

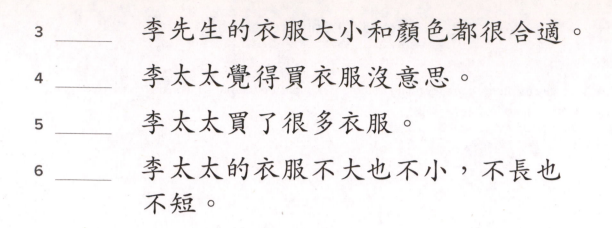

┌─────────────────────────────────┐
│   **Writing and Grammar**   │
└─────────────────────────────────┘

A Write the radical in the character 付 and three characters with the same radical, then provide the meaning of each character in English (write the common radical in 1).

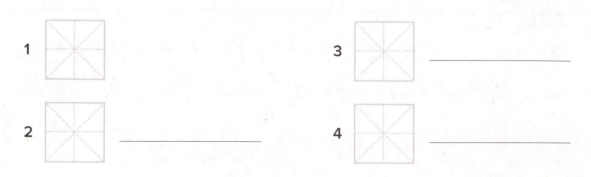

1

2 _____

3 _____

4 _____

B Draw a line from each object to its respective measure word. PRESENTATIONAL

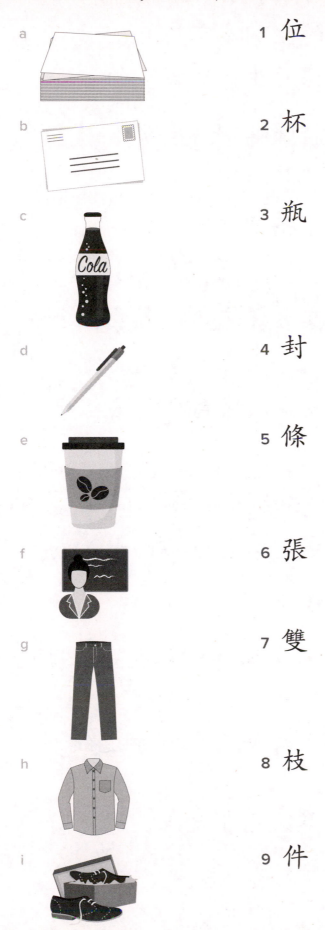

a

b

c

d

e

f

g

h

i

1 位

2 杯

3 瓶

4 封

5 條

6 張

7 雙

8 枝

9 件

C Answer these questions using "挺…的," following the example below. **INTERPERSONAL**

Q: 你覺得這一課的生詞多不多？

A: 我覺得（這一課的生詞）挺多的。

1 Q: 白英愛覺得王朋帥嗎？

A: _____

2 Q: 王朋覺得李友漂亮嗎？

A: _____

3 Q: 常老師覺得李友念課文念得怎麼樣？

A: _____

4 Q: 常老師覺得李友寫漢字寫得怎麼樣？

A: _____

D Rewrite these sentences using "A 跟 B 一樣 + adj," following the example below. **PRESENTATIONAL**

高文中今年十八歲，李友今年也十八歲。

高文中跟李友一樣大。

1 這件襯衫是中號的，那件襯衫也是中號的。

_____

2 這雙鞋五十塊錢，那雙鞋也五十塊錢。

_____

3 學中文很酷，學英文也很酷。

_____

4 這個教室很新，那個教室也很新。

_____

5 紐約很有意思，北京也很有意思。

_____

E Based on the information provided, complete this conversation between a salesperson and a customer. PRESENTATIONAL

售貨員：_____?

李小姐：我想買一條褲子。

售貨員：_____?

李小姐：大號的。

售貨員：這條太大了，您可以換 _____。

李小姐：中號的長短、大小都很合適。

售貨員：_____?

李小姐：還要買一雙鞋。

售貨員：_____?

李小姐：黃的。

售貨員：一條褲子十九塊，一雙鞋十五塊，
　　　　一共 _____。

李小姐：能不能 _____?

售貨員：對不起，我們不收＿＿＿＿＿＿＿＿＿＿。

李小姐：＿＿＿＿＿＿＿＿＿＿＿＿＿＿＿＿＿。

售貨員：找您六十六塊。

F Translate these sentences into Chinese. PRESENTATIONAL

1 Student A: This store is quite nice. Their clothes aren't too expensive.

_____

Student B: Although their clothes aren't too expensive, they don't take credit cards. That's so inconvenient.

_____

_____

2 Student A: What size shirt do you wear?

_____

Student B: I wear medium.

_____

Student A: Do you like this red one? The style and the color are both right (for you).

_____

_____

Student B: I'll try it on.

_____

Student A: It's a little big (on you).

_____

Student B: Let's get a size small.

_____

3 **Student A:** I like to go shopping with my sister. She pays. I don't have to (pay).

_____

_____

Student B: Is that so? Your sister is so nice.

_____

4 **Student A:** I'd like to buy some pens. How much is this kind of pen?

_____

_____

Student B: Three dollars each.

_____

Student A: Why so expensive? How about that kind?

_____

Student B: That kind is as expensive as this kind.

_____

G Write down your comments on a photo of someone that was recently posted on social media. Include details about the fit and color of the clothes he/she is wearing. Indicate whether you like his/her sense of style, and provide some fashion tips. PRESENTATIONAL

_____

_____

_____

_____

_____

H You're shopping for new clothes online. From the items below, choose an outfit. Write a customer review detailing the items you purchased, including their colors, sizes, and prices. Also comment on how you look in your new outfit, how it fits, and if it was too expensive. PRESENTATIONAL

DRESS
$ 120.00
COLORS: black, yellow, red, white
SIZE: 6, 10, 14

SHOES
$ 130.00
COLORS: black, yellow, red, white
SIZE: 6, 10, 14

SHIRT
$ 50.00
COLORS: black, yellow, red, white
SIZE: 6, 10, 14

PANTS
$ 55.00
COLORS: black, yellow, red, white
SIZE: 6, 10, 14

SHORTS
$ 55.00
COLORS: black, yellow, red, white
SIZE: 6, 10, 14

OVERCOAT
$ 120.00
COLORS: black, yellow, red, white
SIZE: 6, 10, 14

_____

_____

_____

_____

_____

交通
Transportation

 Check off the following items as you learn them.

Useful Expressions

[ ] Do you know how to get there?

[ ] Let me drive you home.

[ ] That's too much trouble.

[ ] I'll take the subway.

[ ] Happy New Year!

Cultural Norms

[ ] Modes of transportation

[ ] Popular ridesharing apps

[ ] Common New Year greetings

[ ] Spring Festival traffic

As you progress through the lesson, note other useful expressions and cultural norms you would like to learn.

_____

_____

_____

Dialogue:
Going Home for Winter Vacation

🔊
Audio

Listening Comprehension

A Listen to the Textbook Dialogue audio, then mark these statements true or false. INTERPRETIVE

1 _____ Li You will be leaving on the twenty-first.

2 _____ Li You should reach the airport no later than eight o'clock in the morning.

3 _____ Li You decides not to take a taxi because she thinks it is too expensive.

4 _____ Li You doesn't know how to get to the airport by public transportation.

5 _____ To get to the airport, Li You can take the subway first, then a bus.

6 _____ Li You finally agrees to go to the airport in Wang Peng's car.

B Listen to the Workbook Dialogue audio, then mark these statements true or false. INTERPRETIVE

1 _____ The woman decides to go home for winter break.

2 _____ The man invites the woman to visit his home.

3 _____ The man and the woman will drive to the man's home together.

4 _____ Plane tickets are not expensive.

Pinyin and Tone

A Identify the characters with the same finals (either *u* or *ü*) and write them in *pinyin*.

路　女　綠　租　錄　出　去

1 *u:* _____

2 *ü:* _____

B Compare the tones of these characters. Indicate the tones with 1 (first tone), 2 (second tone), 3 (third tone), 4 (fourth tone), or 0 (neutral tone).

1　公 _____ 共 _____　　4　先 _____ 線 _____

2　者 _____ 這 _____　　5　煩 _____ 飯 _____

3　麻 _____ 媽 _____　　6　汽 _____ 起 _____

Speaking

A Answer these questions in Chinese based on the Textbook Dialogue. PRESENTATIONAL

   1 What is Li You going to do for winter vacation?

   2 What are the two modes of transportation that Li You first considers?

   3 Why does Li You abandon her first two choices?

   4 How does Li You get to the airport in the end?

B In pairs, find out what your partner plans to do for winter break, and what mode of transportation he/she will use. INTERPERSONAL

C Ask your partner the best way to get to the airport from his/her home, and if there are any alternate routes. INTERPERSONAL

Reading Comprehension

A Read this note, then mark the statements true or false. INTERPRETIVE

小李：

　　明天是我的生日，你明天到我家來吃晚飯，怎麼樣？到我家來你可以坐四路公共汽車，也可以坐地鐵，都很方便。坐公共汽車慢，可是不用換車。坐地鐵快，但是得換車，

"Lesson 10 | Transportation 179"

先坐紅線，坐三站，然後換藍線，坐兩站下車
就到了。希望你能來！明天見。

小白

十二月五日下午三點

1 _____ Little Li wants to take Little Bai out to dinner tomorrow.

2 _____ To get to Little Bai's home, it is faster to take the subway than the bus.

3 _____ Little Bai's home is not on a bus route or a subway line.

4 _____ Little Bai's birthday is December 5.

5 _____ Little Bai does not expect her friend to drive tomorrow.

B Read this email, then mark the statements true or false. INTERPRETIVE

小白，你好。我是小高。我昨天才知道你
這個週末要去機場。你告訴王朋了，可是怎麼
沒告訴我呢？你別坐公共汽車去機場。坐公共
汽車不方便，也很慢。你得坐五站，還要換地
鐵，太麻煩了。我可以開車送你到機場去。我
開車開得很好。你今天回宿舍以後給我打個電
話，好嗎？要是你的飛機票已經買了，我想知
道你的飛機是幾點的。好，我等你的電話，
再見。

1 _____ Little Bai will go to the airport today.

2 _____ Wang Peng knows that Little Bai is going to the airport.

3 _____ According to Little Gao, public transportation to the airport is not convenient.

4 _____ Little Gao considers himself a good driver.

5 _____ Little Gao asks Little Bai to wait for his phone call later today.

6 _____ Little Gao knows that Little Bai has already purchased her plane ticket.

C What tickets are sold here? INTERPRETIVE

_____

_____

Writing and Grammar

A Write the *pinyin* for the characters in the top row, compare them with the *pinyin* of the characters below, then consider the relationship between each pair.

1 機 _____   2 漂 _____   3 站 _____   4 紅 _____

幾 *(jǐ)*   票 *(piào)*   占 *(zhàn)*   工 *(gōng)*

B Complete these exchanges by creating topic-comment sentences, following the example below.
PRESENTATIONAL

Student A: 我昨天看了一個外國電影。(I saw that movie, too.)

Student B: 那個電影我也看了。

1 Student A: 你做功課了沒有？(Yes.)

  Student B: _____

2 Student A: 你喜歡不喜歡喝中國茶？(Yes.)

  Student B: _____

3 Student A: 老師給了他一枝筆。(He gave that pen to his friend.)

  Student B: _____

4 Student A: 我昨天去買了一雙鞋。(I don't like that pair.)

  Student B: _____

5 Student A: 我今天認識了一個男孩子。(We all know that boy.)

  Student B: _____

C Fill in the blanks with 或者 or 還是. PRESENTATIONAL

1 老師正在開會_____給學生考試？

2 你覺得坐地鐵方便_____坐公共汽車方便？

3 你想買藍色的，黑色的，_____咖啡色的褲子？

4 今天晚上我想練習發音_____復習語法。

5 我想要一杯咖啡_____一瓶可樂。

D Based on the images, answer the questions using 先⋯再⋯. Follow the example below.
PRESENTATIONAL

Q: 李友今天上什麼課？  followed by

A: 她今天先上中文課，再上電腦課。

1 Q: 王朋週末想怎麼玩兒？ followed by

A: _____

2 Q: 張老師明天得做什麼？ followed by

A: _____

3 Q: 白英愛寒假怎麼回家？ followed by

A: _____

E Make suggestions by using 還是…吧, following the example below. PRESENTATIONAL

Student A: 今天晚上沒事兒，我們看電視，好嗎？
（沒意思，去跳舞）

Student B: 看電視沒意思，我們還是去跳舞吧！

1 Student A: 這件黑色的襯衫很便宜。我想買。
（樣子不好，別買）

Student B: _____

2 Student A: 我想坐公共汽車去機場。
（太麻煩，打車）

Student B: _____

3 Student A: 我們今天晚上去聽音樂會，怎麼樣？
（沒空，明天晚上）

Student B: _____

F Translate these sentences into Chinese. Use the topic-comment sentence structure to translate the bolded text. PRESENTATIONAL

1 Student A: How are we going to get to the airport? By taxi or subway?

_____

Student B: Taxi or subway are both okay.

_____

2 Student A: Give me a ride to school tomorrow, OK?

_____

Student B: Sorry, I'm very busy tomorrow. You'd better take the bus.

_____

3 Student A: I'm flying home this winter break.

_____

Student B: Did you get **the ticket**?

_____

Student A: I got **the ticket** already. It's (a ticket) for December 15.

_____

Student B: On that day, we will have dinner first, and then I'll give you a ride to the airport.

_____

Student A: Really? That would be great. Thank you.

_____

Student B: Don't mention it.

_____

G Little Wang is taking the subway to the airport. Based on the images, describe how he plans to get there from school. PRESENTATIONAL

_____

_____

_____

_____

H It's Little Wang's first time taking the Beijing subway. Little Wang is now at Xizhimen (西直門) station. He has to go to Wangfujing (王府井) to do some shopping. Give him detailed directions based on this subway map (note that Line 4 is 四號線). You can write the names of the stations in _pinyin_. PRESENTATIONAL

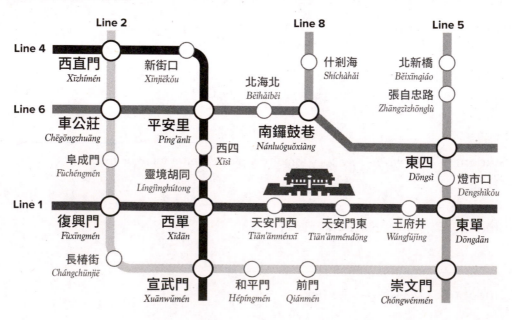

Email: Thanks for the Ride

Listening Comprehension

A Listen to the Textbook Email audio, then mark these statements true or false. INTERPRETIVE

1 _____ Wang Peng gives Li You a ride to the airport.

2 _____ Li You cannot drive.

3 _____ Li You's hometown has buses but no subway.

4 _____ Li You has been busy visiting old friends.

5 _____ Li You feels that everybody drives too slowly.

6 _____ Li You is looking forward to hearing from Wang Peng.

B Listen to the Workbook Dialogue 1 audio, then mark these statements true or false. INTERPRETIVE

1 _____ The woman knows how to get to the man's home.

2 _____ To get to the man's home by subway, first take the Green Line, then change to the Blue Line.

3 _____ The woman needs to take three different buses to get to the man's house.

4 _____ The woman decides to take the bus to the man's place.

C Listen to the Workbook Dialogue 2 audio, then mark these statements true or false. INTERPRETIVE

1 _____ The man will be busy tomorrow.

2 _____ The man claims to be a very good driver.

3 _____ The man will go to the airport with the woman.

4 _____ The woman does not have total confidence in the man.

Pinyin and Tone

A Identify the characters with the same initials (either *j* or *zh*) and write them in *pinyin*.

張　機　緊　假　站　件　者　己

1 *j:* _____

2 *zh:* _____

Compare the tones of these characters. Indicate the tones with 1 (first tone), 2 (second tone), 3 (third tone), 4 (fourth tone), or 0 (neutral tone).

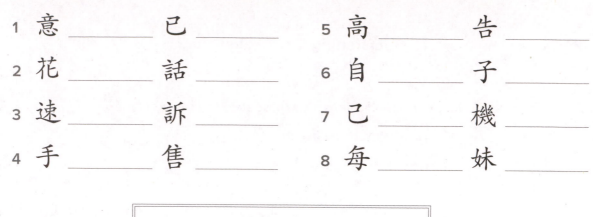

1 意 _____ 已 _____   5 高 _____ 告 _____

2 花 _____ 話 _____   6 自 _____ 子 _____

3 速 _____ 訴 _____   7 己 _____ 機 _____

4 手 _____ 售 _____   8 每 _____ 妹 _____

Speaking

A Answer these questions based on the Textbook Email. PRESENTATIONAL

1 How do you express New Year greetings in Chinese?

2 Why does Li You thank Wang Peng?

3 What has Li You been doing the past few days?

4 Is Li You a good driver? Explain.

B In pairs, role-play calling and thanking your friend for driving you to the airport. Describe what you've been doing since you returned home, and wish your friend a happy New Year. INTERPERSONAL

C Explain how to get to the airport from your friend's house by referring to the image below. PRESENTATIONAL

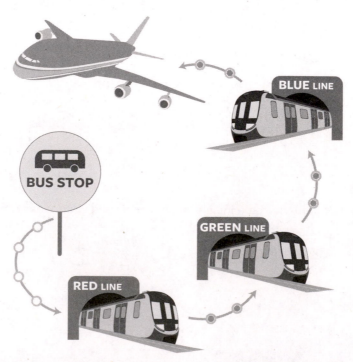

A Read this diary entry, then mark the statements true or false. INTERPRETIVE

小李的一篇日記

今天我開車去小張家找他玩兒。高速公路上的汽車很多，都開得很快。我不知道小張家怎麼走，就看手機上的地圖。因為在高速公路上開車讓我很緊張，所以我開車開得特別慢，很晚才到小張家。

1 _____ Little Li visited Little Zhang because they wanted to study together.

2 _____ Little Li is a skilled highway driver.

3 _____ Little Li had no difficulties finding Little Zhang's place.

4 _____ Little Li was probably grateful that she had her cell phone with her.

5 _____ Little Li got to Little Zhang's place late because her car is old.

B Read this passage, then mark the statements true or false. INTERPRETIVE

弟弟今天開車送媽媽去機場。高速公路上汽車很多，開得都很快，弟弟很緊張，所以開得特別慢。媽媽的飛機是兩點半的，他們三點才到機場。機場的人告訴媽媽，她只能坐明天的飛機了。弟弟很不好意思，說明天再開車送媽媽去機場。可是媽媽說她明天還是自己坐出租汽車吧。

1 _____ My brother is a very experienced driver.

2 _____ The traffic on the highway was light, so people drove fast.

3 _____ My brother drove very slowly because he was nervous.

4 _____ When my brother and mother arrived at the airport, her flight had departed.

5 _____ There were later flights today, but my mother preferred to wait until tomorrow.

6 _____ My mother will most likely not ride in the same car to the airport tomorrow.

Read this passage, then answer the questions in English. INTERPRETIVE

在中國，小孩都特別喜歡中國新年，因為他們可以穿新衣，穿新鞋，爸爸媽媽也給他們錢。不過，李小紅告訴我她不喜歡中國新年。她三十歲，有先生，可是沒有孩子，所以別人不給她錢，她得給別人的小孩很多錢。李小紅還說新年的時候公共汽車很少，她自己也沒有車，所以出去玩也不方便。她覺得中國新年太沒意思了。

1　Which two Chinese New Year traditions make children happy? Explain in detail.

_____

2　Which two Chinese New Year traditions make Li Xiaohong unhappy? Explain in detail.

_____

3　Is Li Xiaohong male or female? How do you know?

_____

D The following are directions to a theme park. Identify at least three means of transportation that tourists can use to get there. INTERPRETIVE

自行開車
花蓮縣壽豐鄉台11線10公里處。

飛　　機
台北　遠東、復興航空公司，
航程約35分鐘。
台中　華信航空公司，航程約1小時。
高雄　遠東、華信航空公司，
航程約 50分鐘。

鐵　　路
台北　觀光列車由台北專車直達
花蓮新站，約需3小時半。
台中　經由台北轉由北迴鐵路直達。
高雄　經南迴鐵路由東部幹線北上抵達。

公　　路
大有巴士客運專車直達花蓮市區後，
轉搭花蓮客運往台東、豐濱方向。

市區公車
花蓮舊火車站發車往台東方向經海岸線。

_____

_____

A Write the common radical and the characters, then provide their meanings in English. Consider their relationship with the radical.

送　速　這　近　道　邊

1 _____

2 _____

3 _____

4 _____

5 _____

6 _____

7 _____

B Based on the images, describe what makes Li You nervous. PRESENTATIONAL

什麼讓李友緊張？

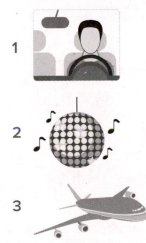

1 _____

2 _____

3 _____

Answer these questions according to your own circumstances. **INTERPERSONAL**

1 什麼讓你緊張？

_____

2 什麼讓你高興？

_____

3 什麼讓你不好意思？

_____

D Answer these questions with 每⋯⋯都⋯⋯, following the example below. **PRESENTATIONAL**

Q: 他<u>晚上</u>看電視嗎？

A: 他每天晚上都看電視。

1 Q: 她<u>早上</u>走高速公路嗎？

A: _____

2 Q: 考試的時候<u>哪一個學生</u>很緊張？

A: _____

3 Q: 常老師<u>哪個週末</u>回家？

A: _____

4 Q: 那個商店的<u>什麼衣服</u>很貴？

A: _____

E Translate these sentences into Chinese. **PRESENTATIONAL**

1 Student A: You speak Chinese so well. How do you normally prepare for your Chinese class?

_____

_____

Student B: I listen to the audio every morning.

_____

2 **Student A:** We'll have dinner first, then we'll go dancing. My treat!

_____

Student B: I feel bad about making you spend money.

_____

3 **Student A:** I'll give you a ride to school today.

_____

Student B: Never mind. I'd better take the bus.

_____

Student A: Why?

_____

Student B: You drive too fast, and it makes me nervous.

_____

Student A: Is that so?

_____

4 **Student A:** I like New York. This city is so interesting.

_____

Student B: I also think New York is quite nice. Its subway is especially convenient.

_____

5 **Student A:** Do you know how to send text messages in Chinese?

_____

Student B: Yes. I send messages in Chinese to my Chinese friends.

_____

Student A: Really? Cool.

_____

Student B: Everybody knows how. I'll teach you.

_____

Student A: Great! New Year is coming. I want to message my friends and wish them a happy New Year.

_____

_____

Student B: OK, I'll teach you now.

_____

F Comment on your city and highway driving skills. If you don't drive, comment on people's driving habits in your city or its public transportation system. PRESENTATIONAL

_____

_____

_____

_____

G The holiday season is approaching. Email or send a text message to your friends in Chinese. Ask them how they are doing and wish them a happy New Year. PRESENTATIONAL

_____

_____

_____

_____

Bringing It Together (Lessons 6–10)

Pinyin and Tone

A Compare the characters' pronunciation and tones, then write them in *pinyin*.

1 喜歡 _____   希望 _____

2 告訴 _____   高速 _____

3 聽錄音 _____   換綠線 _____

4 多少錢 _____   都是錢 _____

5 售貨員 _____   或者 _____

Radicals

A Group these characters according to their radicals.

客　得　筆　慢　錯　然　詞　線　貴
衫　錢　澡　等　室　貨　煩　襯　宿　綠
讓　很　練　緊　語　懂　襯　律　笑
員　第　鐵　褲　汽　念　照　洗　試

Radical　　　**Characters**

1 _____　_____

2 _____　_____

3 _____　_____

4 _____　_____

5 _____

6 _____

7 _____

8 _____

9 _____

10 _____

11 _____

VO Compounds

A Circle the verbs that are VO compounds.

學習 知道 開會 寫字

告訴 付錢 坐地鐵 下車

說話 預習

Communication

A Ask your classmates the following questions about school life. Jot down their answers, then report to the class on who has the most in common with you.

1 你是大學幾年級的學生？

_____

2 你的專業是什麼？_____

3 你這個學期上什麼課？

_____

4 你每天有幾節課？ _____

5 你最喜歡上什麼課？

_____

6 你最不喜歡上什麼課？

_____

7 你的考試多不多？ _____

8 你什麼課考試考得最好？

_____

B In pairs, ask and answer the following questions about studying Chinese. Present an oral or written report to your class based on the information you collect.

1 你為什麼學中文？

_____

2 你覺得學中文有意思嗎？

_____

3 你常常跟誰一起練習說中文？

_____

4 你去老師的辦公室問問題嗎？

_____

5 你覺得每課的生詞多不多？語法難不難？

_____

6 你平常先聽錄音再練習漢字還是先練習漢字再聽錄音？

_____

7 你平常上新課以前預習嗎？

_____

8 你平常考試以前找誰幫你復習？

_____

9 你平常考試考得怎麼樣？

_____

10 你覺得你的老師說話說得快不快？

_____

11 你覺得你寫漢字寫得怎麼樣？

_____

12 你會不會用中文發短信、寫信、寫日記或者寫電子郵件？

_____

C Ask your friend the following questions to find the perfect birthday gift.

1 你希望有件新襯衫，有條新褲子，還是有雙新鞋？

_____

2 你（不）喜歡什麼顏色？

_____

3 襯衫你穿多大的？ _____

4 褲子你穿幾號的？鞋呢？

_____

5 你希望我自己去買，還是你跟我一起去買？

_____

6 要是大小、長短不合適，你希望我幫你去
商店換，還是你自己去換？

_____

D Before getting in a car with your friend, ask him/her the following questions.

1 你會開車嗎？ _____

2 要是你昨天晚上沒睡覺，你能開車嗎？

_____

3 你的車新不新？ _____

4 你開車開得怎麼樣？ _____

5 你常常一邊開車，一邊打手機嗎？

_____

6 你在高速公路上開車緊張不緊張？

_____

7 要是你的車有問題，我們坐公共汽車還是打車？

_____